Structuring the Group Experience

A Guide to the Design and Leadership of
Psychoeducational Groups

SUSAN R. FURR

American
Counseling
Association
counseling.org

American Counseling Association
2461 Eisenhower Avenue, Suite 300
Alexandria, Viriginia 22314

Published in the United States of America

Library of Congress Cataloging-in-Publication Data

Names: Furr, Susan R. author
Title: Structuring the group experience : a guide to the design andleadership of psychoeducational
   groups / Susan R. Furr.
Description: Alexandria, VA : American Counseling Association, [2026] |Includes bibliographical
   references. | Summary: "An all-encompassing guide for designing and executing your own
   psychoeducational groups, this book is as practical as it is thorough. From introducing the group
   dynamic, to creating curricula that utilizes well-conceived content and activities, it offers a step-by-
   step guide for developing a group that fosters the knowledge and skills necessary for client growth
   and development. Designed to be used again and again, this is a resource for everyone from students
   looking for hands-on guidance to practitioners wanting to sharpen their skillset"-- Provided by
   publisher.
Identifiers: LCCN 2025036668 | ISBN 9781556200281
Subjects: LCSH: Group counseling | Group relations training
Classification: LCC BF636.7.G76 F87 2026
LC record available at https://lccn.loc.gov/2025036668

I am grateful for the continued support and encouragement from all my family—Ted, Kasey, James, Alex, and Emily, as well as our additions, Audrey and Logan.

Contents

Preface

I began my journey of leading structured groups during my first counseling position in a middle school. My principal had purchased a DUSO kit (Developing Understanding of Self and Others) to use when working with sixth grade students as they transitioned to middle school. My group counseling course had not included much instruction about leading structured groups, given that the Association of Specialists in Group Work did not, at that time, have the Guiding Principles that we use today. I was thrilled to use the DUSO kit with students. It included a manual, story books, puppets, role-playing cards, and group discussion cards. With the kit, I found that students were more focused and engaged than they were in open-ended counseling groups.

When I returned to graduate school, I had the good fortune to work with Dr. John Galassi, who was writing and publishing in the area of assertion training and had completed a guide for an assertion training program. During this time, I developed a strong collaboration with Dr. Katherine Fulkerson. We were tasked with providing assertion training through the university's community education program. As we evolved our group content, we began to develop guidelines for how to design effective groups which included content, activities, and methods to process the meaning that members gained from group interactions. This early work provided the foundation for this manual. I am forever grateful for the contributions of Dr. Fulkerson to my understanding of the value of designing effective structured groups.

My exposure to and work with structured groups deepened during my time as a student intern at the university counseling center at the University of North Carolina at Chapel Hill. At the center, interns were given ample opportunity to lead structured groups. When I was accepted for a predoctoral internship in counseling psychology at the University of Texas at Austin, I studied under the leadership of Dr. David Drum, a prolific scholar of structured groups and creator of the Clearinghouse for Structured Group Programs. Along with colleagues Dr. Alice Lawler and Dr. Adrienne Barna, we continued to evolve our skills in this mode of counseling and enjoyed this process because of their clear purpose and effectiveness.

During my years working as a counseling psychologist at the University of North Carolina at Charlotte's counseling center, I led multiple structured groups each semester. I began to truly value the growth students gained from this modality of treatment. Because I also had an academic appointment in the graduate counseling program, I was asked to teach courses on a regular basis. When the Council for Accreditation of Counseling and Related Educational Programs (CACREP) evolved counseling programs to include 60 credit hours, our program decided to add a second group course focused on structured groups. Thus, our course on the leadership and design of structured groups was born. I designed this course using the principles presented in this manual. When I moved to a full-time faculty position, I was able to present these concepts to our students and further refine this method. I hope you find this approach useful as you find ways to better equip your clients with the skills needed to meet unique life challenges.

Introduction to Structured Groups

Throughout its history as a counseling modality, the structured group has evolved to encompass a variety of forms. Originally, groups were viewed as means either to provide mental health services to a larger number of individuals than traditional one-on-one counseling sessions or to collectively support people facing similar issues. Although not a substitute for individual counseling, group work can provide resources that are not present in individual therapeutic interventions. The 1990 revision of the Association of Specialists for Group Work's (ASGW) *Professional Standards for the Training of Group Workers* defined four distinct group work specializations: (1) task and work group facilitation, (2) psychoeducational groups, (3) group counseling, and (4) group psychotherapy (Wilson et al., 2000). Each type of group has a specialized purpose, and determining which group specialization to pursue should be guided by client needs. Furthermore, the Council for Accreditation of Counseling and Related Educational Programs Standards (CACREP, 2024) requires that entry-level programs include instruction in group counseling that examines these different types of groups (Section 3, Standard F.7).

Psychoeducational groups are a vital form of group intervention in which group members learn specific skills to address life challenges. Often referred to as structured groups, this type of group provides a specific curriculum to help members understand the dynamics of their issues and then develop and practice necessary skills. One difference between a structured group and a counseling group is that the structured group is focused on a specific topic, whereas a counseling group has a more open nature. A structured group follows a predetermined curriculum with limited space for deviation to other topics. Counseling groups may have a specific focus, such as a group about forming healthy relationships, but members generate the group content, rather than the leader creating the content, as they do in structured groups. Additionally, structured groups are generally time-limited in that they may be as brief as four sessions and generally do not exceed ten sessions. Members commit to attending all sessions, and the group does not add members once it begins. Counseling groups often do not have a predetermined number of sessions, and members may leave when they have made satisfactory progress, and new members may join whenever they wish.

To lead a psychoeducational group, a counselor must have knowledge of group theory, basic group dynamics, group process, leadership roles, and the mechanics of beginning a group, all of which are covered in CACREP-accredited group counseling courses. In addition, CACREP Standards require an experiential component for class members, mandating a minimum of "10 clock hours over the course of one academic term" (Section 3, Standard F.10). Although group counseling is a key focus of counseling programs, the coursework tends to conclude when the CACREP Standards have been fulfilled. Group counseling courses often focus on the *specialty* of group counseling, which is grounded in group theory and leadership skills, but they tend to lack guidance regarding how to design a psychoeducational group. Many group counseling textbooks only provide a chapter or two on the topic, with little specific instruction on how to effectively design and deliver the material. For example, Gladding's (2020) textbook about group counseling includes a chapter on the ASGW's four distinct group specializations, which includes psychoeducational groups. In this textbook, Gladding includes chapters that discuss which types of groups to use with specific populations, such as adolescents and older adults, with descriptions of how psychoeducational groups would look with such populations. However, there is limited discussion about how to develop these groups from start to finish. A similar pattern is found in Capuzzi and Stauffer's (2020) textbook, in which one chapter is devoted to the four types of group work. Although these are excellent resources on the process of group counseling, psychoeducational groups specifically are lightly acknowledged, with limited instruction on their design process.

Students develop leadership skills in group counseling courses that can be adapted to leading structured groups. However, because these courses rarely delve deeper than what is required by the CACREP Standards (2024), students often finish the course with a limited understanding of how to develop a dynamic curriculum for a more structured group experience. These groups are increasingly viewed as avenues to dispense information to people, rather than opportunities to utilize the myriad benefits of group dynamics and enact tangible change within group members (Gitterman & Knight, 2016). A well-designed psychoeducational group employs best practices enhanced with creative activities that personalize the experience for group members and tailor the knowledge shared.

One crucial element of structured groups—and one that distinguishes them from counseling groups—is that they prioritize teaching. Psychoeducational groups establish specific goals and build content that is derived from these goals. While counseling groups may have a general focus—such as a group emphasizing relationship issues—a psychoeducational group has specific teaching modules on relationships followed by activities to help members develop appropriate skills. In a structured group, clients learn content and concepts that can be translated outside of sessions into practices that change thoughts, feelings, and behaviors. The counseling process becomes an art when it combines this information and experiential learning in practical ways that group members can apply to their lives outside of the group.

Why Choose a Structured Group Approach?

According to the World Health Organization (WHO, 2004), in order to live a healthy and meaningful life, it is important to reduce risk factors and strengthen protective factors. One way to do this is through evidence-based structured programs that help improve emotional knowledge and increase problem-solving skills. Mental health professionals, with their wide range of knowledge about the skills and understanding needed to live a healthy life, are critical to this endeavor. Structured groups, which foster coping skills and can remediate deficits in learning, are an important resource for counselors and clients seeking a healthy and meaningful life (Sachs & Erfurth, 2021; Terrazas-Carrillo & Garcia, 2024; Usta & Aygin, 2020). Clients who engage with structured groups can gain perspective and understanding about the problematic areas of their lives. This, in turn, can support skills development and ultimately improve quality of life.

Independently developing a repertoire of positive living skills can be a challenge for some individuals. According to social learning theory, people learn skills through observing and imitating the behavior of others (Bandura et al., 1977). When an environment is rich in positive role models, individuals can learn coping and performance skills by monitoring their behaviors and implementing them in similar situations. External rewards and internal reinforcement, such as feelings of success, can motivate individuals to mimic behaviors. When one's environment does not include successful role models, one might miss out on appropriate behaviors for imitation. To compound that, the rise of social media may be a major influence on the behaviors of youth as compared to in vivo models. For example, Hendriks et al. (2021) found that reading posts about alcohol use on social media led to increased alcohol use the following day. Social media tends to glamorize alcohol use by only showing the positive social aspects, while excluding any negative aspects. Structured groups can mitigate risks like those posed by social media by teaching clients how to evaluate and question potentially biased or one-sided external content and presenting content and models that build positive coping skills.

Learning is unreliable by nature and can go awry at multiple points in development. Structured groups are useful supplements to traditional learning because they can be designed to address all levels of intervention. These groups offer a constructive approach for intervening at the levels of primary prevention, secondary prevention, and even tertiary prevention. These structured group experiences can either be standalone interventions or serve as adjuncts to individual counseling or psychotherapy. In the following section, the three levels of prevention are described, with examples of how structured groups have been implemented for intervention. The examples demonstrate a wide array of topics that can be addressed using a psychoeducational model. In addition, they demonstrate the variety of client issues that can be met in a structured group, ranging from clients seeking personal growth to clients facing complex mental health problems. Although the content of the groups differs, the method presented can be used to design groups for almost any population. Leaders of psychoeducational groups can develop groups that help address anticipated problems (primary prevention), problems that have created adjustment issues (secondary prevention), or issues that have a long history of interfering with daily living (tertiary prevention).

Primary Prevention

The WHO (2004) has emphasized that focusing on the prevention of mental health disorders is one of the most effective ways to reduce their burden. Resilience-building interventions, wherein individuals learn how to cope with challenging situations before they occur, are productive mitigating factors (Skeffington et al., 2013). Primary prevention is defined as identifying susceptible individuals and providing intervention that either limits the risks or increases capacity for addressing the issue they face (Singh et al., 2022).

Structured groups offer a useful avenue for primary prevention. For example, college students who participated in a four-week resilience intervention group demonstrated improved coping strategies, higher scores on protective factors, and lower levels of symptomatology when compared to a waitlist control group (Steinhardt & Dolbier, 2008). Thomas and Looney (2004) found that in a study focusing on pregnant and parenting adolescents, participating in a comprehensive psychoeducational group helped these adolescents change their parenting attitudes and beliefs, which suggested "an ultimate improvement in health promotion and disease prevention."

Primary prevention has also been effective in elementary and middle school settings. Shapiro et al. (2002) found that students in grades four through eight self-reported and teacher-reported reduced aggression when their teachers were trained to deliver a structured guidance curriculum focused on violence prevention. Though not specifically a structured group, this primary prevention effort followed a psychoeducational curriculum, similar to one that might be used in a structured group. Results also indicated a school-wide decrease in aggression-related disciplinary incidents and suspensions for aggression (Shapiro et al., 2002). Another effective program is Signs of Suicide (SOS). High school students who participated in the small group structured program exhibited increased knowledge about suicide risks and depression and reduced self-reported suicide attempts (Volungis, 2020). Extrapolating from these examples, counselors have demonstrated the ability to identify potential difficulties a population may encounter and then design interventions that can help individuals master the skills needed to successfully navigate the challenge.

Secondary Prevention

The goal of secondary prevention is early detection. This approach often takes place through screenings to detect issues in early stages (Keyes et al., 2025). For example, researchers found psychoeducation to be helpful to families after a family member's first psychotic experience (Tapias et al., 2021). Psychoeducation improved families' understanding of their afflicted relatives' conditions and reduced isolation and stigma. Psychoeducational groups have also helped children of parents who have a mental illness. This issue is particularly important given that these children have a higher risk of developing mental health issues if they are not given tools for coping (Tapias et al., 2021). In a similar study, family members of someone with a mental illness who engaged in a group program made significant improvements in their understanding of said illness and its treatment (Day et al., 2017). In a comprehensive literature review, group psychoeducation is effective in preventing relapse in bipolar disorder (Bond & Anderson, 2015).

Schools have several opportunities in which to offer secondary prevention via psychoeducational group work. De Jonge-Heesen et al. (2020) found that implementing a cognitive-behavior-focused group for students with self-reported depressive symptoms resulted in significant symptom reduction. Research has also demonstrated that students with risk factors can significantly increase psychological resilience and significantly decrease irrational beliefs through applying a cognitive behavior therapy approach in psychoeducational groups (Şahin & Türk, 2021). Such results indicate that schools can screen for mental health issues and deliver interventions to strengthen the mental health of their students through implementing content-based groups. Such groups can prevent the development of more serious mental health issues.

Tertiary Prevention

The purpose of tertiary prevention is to limit the impact of a significant life event or health condition. At the point of tertiary prevention, symptoms have already appeared (Keyes et al., 2025). Psychoeducational groups focused on tertiary prevention aim to reduce the impact and ease the effects of the impacting event or mental health issue.

Research has demonstrated that psychoeducational groups can be an effective intervention for those dealing with the challenges of serious mental health issues and can help individuals develop skills to moderate the impacts of their illness. An example of tertiary prevention is a psychoeducational group designed for veterans who have attempted suicide (Gebhardt et al., 2022). In this group, psychoeducation consisted of understanding one's own suicidal experiences, developing skills to reduce risks, and building strategies to target influencing factors. The group format helped participants feel less alone in facing their suicidal thoughts and behaviors.

Bipolar disorder displays psychiatric therapeutic complexity and needs a comprehensive approach that complements pharmacotherapy. Valls et al. (2022) found that participants in a ten-week psychoeducational group at an outpatient clinic improved their general psychosocial functioning and demonstrated reduced depressive symptoms when compared to a treatment-as-usual group.

A psychoeducational group designed for those diagnosed with a substance use disorder found significantly lower rates of relapse for those in the treatment group when compared to the control group. Those in the treatment group displayed significantly higher scores on perceived wellness, social functioning, and coping after the group and at the three-month follow-up (Kargin & Hicdurmaz, 2020).

As these examples demonstrate, whether used as a standalone approach or as support to individual counseling, an educational approach focused on learning new skills and understanding—in other words, a structured group—can enhance mental health functioning.

Group Dynamics

One of the greatest errors a leader of a psychoeducational group can make is to ignore the power of group dynamics. They may focus on the content and "teaching" aspects of the group without considering the group dynamics. Content is important—clients often are missing key information about healthy ways to address their issues—and helping professionals are obligated to share knowledge about changing the thoughts and behaviors that fuel destructive emotions. However, limiting clinical practice to sharing information is not enough to foster growth. Self-help books would "cure" all ills if lack of knowledge were the only factor causing problems. Information sharing is a strategic aspect of structured groups, but a group's effectiveness is determined by how that information is processed and integrated by its members. Groups need to teach the content and then go further by processing it so that members can personalize the meaning of this new knowledge in their own lives (Gitterman & Knight, 2016).

Group Therapy Factors

Yalom (1995), an expert on group dynamics, identified the therapeutic factors that make groups a powerful treatment modality. Although he identified these factors through his work with psychotherapy groups, leaders of psychoeducational groups can draw from the importance of these principles.

Instillation of Hope

The instillation of hope is easily integrated into the structured group model (Yalom, 1995). Group members need to believe that the group process will work for them. This factor starts with the leader. The group leader must believe the group content will contribute to each client's growth. If a client has hope that the group process will work, then they will be more committed and willing to participate. This process can begin early, starting with the advertising of the group and screening of group members. Understanding that the group has been designed to mitigate an issue that a potential client is facing creates hope that, by participating in the group, members can find relief. Because the group has clearly identified goals and objectives, potential members can see that positive outcomes are possible. If the leader has previous experience with clients who have benefited from the group experience, the leader can share how the process has worked for others. The leader's attitude about the group design and process is key to the group's success.

Universality

In American culture and society, mental health issues are often kept private due to a sense of shame. According to Yalom (1995), clients may fear they are unique in their negative experiences and are afraid of displaying this side to others. In this age of digital communication, in which only the best life experiences are posted and shared, one may fear that they can never be as good as others. The fear of inadequacy is often the secret they are keeping from others.

The group experience is a safe environment for facades to fall, allowing members' deeper concerns to be revealed. In this process, members can begin to realize that they are not unique in their concerns and, therefore, feel a sense of acceptance among those who share similar issues. A sense of relief emerges from seeing others facing similar challenges. Psychoeducational groups can embrace the power of universality due to the focused topic of the group. All members attend a given group for similar reasons, leading to an easy connection among members. In a group I led on coping with eating disorders, two members recognized each other from mutual classes and were surprised that the other person was there. They each viewed the other as highly capable and confident and assumed the other person had no issues. This encounter provided an opening to discuss the complexity of people, how strengths and challenges coexist, and the importance of not defining oneself by a diagnosis.

Because structured groups have a specific focus, this dynamic of universality comes naturally. For example, I found that in my group on building self-esteem, members automatically connected over how they allow their negative thoughts to interfere with what they want to accomplish in their lives. The common focus of the group allows for immediate bonding due to the mutual purpose of being in the group.

Imparting of Information

Yalom (1995) observed that members learned from each other and the leader both implicitly and explicitly. Psychoeducational groups embrace teaching as a central part of the group and use both direct instruction and sharing among group members as important strategies. While most learning in groups is implicit, Yalom acknowledged that groups have also embraced explicit knowledge. Learning about symptoms and contributing factors can be an important foundation for making specific changes. For example, understanding the physiological aspects of panic disorder provides a foundation on which one can develop skills to change cognitive triggers and employ breathing techniques to reduce the impact of episodes. Learning this information in the presence of others who share similar challenges can provide support for incorporating the skills.

Yalom (1995) also observed that implicit learning occurred in groups when sharing advice. While he viewed this activity as one that distracted the group from deeper emotional work, he did observe that members, through offering advice, demonstrated that they cared about each other. That mutual care was beneficial to the group dynamic. However, for advice-giving to be helpful, direct suggestions must be avoided. Providing alternatives that a person can consider in terms of the outcome they desire is the best way for members to collaborate on solutions.

Altruism

Often, clients enter counseling with the belief that they have nothing worthwhile to offer others. One of the benefits of working within a group framework is the opportunity for members to give to other members. In Yalom's (1995) view, altruism refers to an individual's desire to feel that they are needed and useful. Members gain a boost to their self-esteem by participating in the interactive process of giving and receiving. They can realize that they have something of worth to offer and are worthy of the gifts that others offer them.

The group setting provides the opportunity for altruism to develop in a way not afforded in individual counseling. This dynamic can be facilitated in psychoeducational groups through the intentional structuring of group activities. By actively pairing two (dyads) or three (triads) members, members can share ideas and engage in problem-solving to mutually help each other. These smaller subgroups also give each member a chance to contribute to another member without fearing judgment from the larger group. Leaders need to consciously plan activities to foster these interactions and teach members how to give constructive feedback. For example, a group on building self-esteem may have a session in which members are separated into dyads and triads and instructed to give and receive compliments. Such an activity should take place after several sessions to ensure that the group members have become more acquainted with each other so that the compliments come from a genuine place of deep understanding. If this activity occurs too early, compliments may feel superficial and lack depth. Learning to give compliments helps members see that they have something to offer. Learning to receive compliments allows members to understand their own worth. This activity also emphasizes that compliments are gifts to be cherished and valued.

The Corrective Recapitulation of the Primary Family Group

Yalom (1995) observed that, occasionally, group members interact with leaders and other group members similarly to how they may interact with family. This allows for past conflicts to be re-experienced with the opportunity to correct their reactions. Most psychoeducational groups are brief in nature, so these familial behaviors are not observed often. However, in long-term group experiences, these behaviors become more common. Over time, issues of jealousy, competition, defiance, and power may emerge among group members, likely stemming from unfinished business in their respective families. There are many initiating events in a group that can prompt these issues. For example, envy may evolve if a group member is also an individual client of the group leader. This member may feel a special bond with the leader, expecting preferential treatment, or sharing "inside" information garnered from their individual sessions. If there is no alternative psychoeducational group led by a different leader, the leader needs to process what the group experience will entail and discuss boundaries for how they will interact with the client. While the counselor is bound by confidentiality to not share their therapeutic relationship, the client has no such restraints. When I was in a similar situation, I found it helpful to limit individual sessions during the time my clients were engaged in my structured groups. My clients needed to be emotionally stable and ready to benefit from new learning. Setting boundaries with existing clients for how to communicate concerning individual issues is important. Use of electronic updates or a brief meeting outside of group time may need to be defined. Clients seemed to appreciate these boundaries and were comforted by the knowledge that their private information remained private.

Development of Socializing Techniques

Working on issues in a group setting is conducive to developing social skills. Even in unstructured counseling groups, members learn to listen to others and give responses in respectful ways. In the group setting, members receive valuable feedback regarding how they are perceived by others and gain insight about how their communication style affects social interactions. Learning to operate within the bounds of the established group rules can be developmental: it teaches group members valuable communication skills. Yalom (1995) even viewed the informal conversations before and after psychotherapy group sessions as important aspects of developing social skills. Children can learn important skills, such as taking turns and waiting to speak, with tools like a talking stick to designate who can speak.

In psychoeducational groups, these same principles apply. The leader may use "rounds" to check in with members and their experiences from the previous week. Members may work in smaller subgroups (dyads or triads) to allow more time for social interactions. But psychoeducational groups can be more intentional about how social skills are incorporated through planning activities based on social interactions. Perhaps the focus of the group is to improve social interactions or assertion training, which enables members to evaluate their current communication style and develop positive ways of expressing their needs and emotions using techniques such as role-playing. Other examples of social-skills-focused groups are improving couples' communication, developing leadership skills, and building friendships. Whether an explicit goal of the group or an implicit byproduct of group activities, structured groups encourage social skills development.

Imitative Behavior

People learn by watching others, and the counseling experience is no exception. Clients often imitate their counselor. In groups, both the leader and other members provide models to emulate (Söchting, 2014). The American Psychological Association (APA, n.d.) defined spectator therapy as "the beneficial effect on group-therapy members of observing the therapy of fellow members with similar or related problems." Vicarious learning, "the acquisition of information, skills, or behavior through watching the performance of others," can be a powerful influence in issue-focused psychoeducational groups (APA, n.d.). Leaders, operating from a place of authority, are the prime models for a group and, as such, they need to be aware of how they present to members.

As a leader, I experienced this in my work with a group on building self-esteem, in which we discussed healthy ways of accepting compliments. Members had the opportunity to practice both giving and receiving compliments, and we spent time processing what it was like to accept a compliment. After the session, a member stopped to say she thought I did a good job in the session. I deferred, explaining that it was really the members who had done the good work. In a light-hearted manner, she replied, saying, "You are just supposed to say 'thank you' and accept the compliment." Even if it's not always this obvious, members do listen to the points that we make and expect us to practice what we teach.

In psychoeducational groups, behavior change is often the goal. Leaders may provide examples of the target behavior so that members understand the components of the behavior. The leader may also demonstrate an example of inappropriate behavior and ask members to identify what is wrong about that behavior. Leaders then demonstrate the appropriate behavior and divide the group into dyads and triads so members can identify key components to practice and role-play the behaviors themselves. Leaders need to emphasize the distinctions between the two demonstrations so members can fully understand the behaviors they are striving to emulate. In my group on assertion training, I demonstrated what I considered to be aggressive behavior, but members misinterpreted it as assertive behavior. Because of that confusion, we examined the differences in the language, gestures, and tone of voice between aggressive and assertive behaviors, and members learned how to differentiate them. With a more careful behavior demonstration, this problem could have been avoided. It may be helpful for leaders to create video demonstrations to analyze for clarity before group sessions.

Leaders also need to monitor interactions among group members while they are practicing skills with each other to ensure members understand the components of the target skills. Observing the small groups to reinforce appropriate behaviors while helping to modify inaccurate responses ensures that members leave the session incorporating positive behavior change. Practicing behavior change in structured groups is beneficial because members are in a safe environment to try new skills and correct any misunderstandings without fear of real-life repercussions.

Interpersonal Learning

Yalom (1995) stressed interpersonal learning, or learning about oneself and others, as another therapeutic force in group work. Moreover, he described three concepts within interpersonal learning. The first is the importance of interpersonal relationships. Group members learn by comparing their perceptions of others with the other members' perceptions. Often, problems result from misperceptions one holds about a significant person in their life. Group members may offer alternative ways to view the other person's actions or motivations. This type of exchange can be built into the structure of a psychoeducational group in which members exchange perceptions and either validate or provide alternative views of how the members have conceptualized the situation.

Yalom's (1995) second concept is the corrective emotional experience. Within the group, members can share emotional situations they have been unable to manage in the past. In sharing what may be a strong emotional response, the member receives support from the group for taking the risk to share and be authentic while also discovering from the other members the appropriateness of their response. Through this reality testing, the affected member can reflect on their perceptions and evaluate whether their response was valid or needs to be adjusted. This type of dynamic usually occurs in long-term groups in which strong emotions are elicited and is not likely to evolve in a psychoeducational group. However, the setting can be structured to help members share alternative ways of viewing situations, which can help modify perceptions that in turn influence emotional reactions.

Yalom's (1995) third concept is the group as a social microcosm. Given enough time in a group, members begin to interact with each other the same way as they interact with others outside of the group. Because this process takes time to evolve, it is less likely to occur in a psychoeducational group. Yet leaders do need to observe patterns of interaction demonstrated among members. For example, a member of a group focused on anger management may show impatience with another member when role-playing ways to respond to a frustrating situation. The leader could use this situation to get the small group to practice the coping skills they have been learning.

Group Cohesiveness

Yalom defined cohesiveness as "the attractiveness of the group for its members," or the comforting feeling of belonging to a group (Yalom & Leszcz, 2020, p. 36). Within this, he included the relationship of the members to the leader(s), as well as the relationships among members. Group cohesiveness can be comparable to the relationship formed in individual counseling. As such, it is not just a therapeutic factor but also a necessary precondition for an effective group. Leaders facilitate cohesiveness by encouraging affective sharing about self, followed by acceptance from other members. Leaders may need to serve as models for how to compassionately and nonjudgmentally respond to this sharing. Although psychoeducational groups are not focused on deep emotional sharing, the fact that members share a common concern may help build cohesiveness. Given the brief nature of structured groups, group cohesion may be limited.

Catharsis

Open expression of affect is a vital part of group work, but is not enough for change by itself. It must be interwoven with other processes, such as cognitive awareness. Reflecting on one's emotional experience in the context of caring for others can prompt change. Because of the structured nature of psychoeducational groups, catharsis is not encouraged. Yet members may experience some emotional relief just by admitting they have an issue, such as low self-esteem, to others who share a similar issue.

Existential Factors

Yalom (1995) emphasized the importance of members recognizing they ultimately must take responsibility for their own lives. Even when one is close to others, there is a realization that they must face life on their own. Participating in a supportive group allows members to embrace their own possibilities. In general, psychoeducational groups are brief, which may limit members' discovery of this factor. However, some groups may explicitly focus on existential issues. I recall a student who designed a career group for midlife career changers. She titled the group "Will Work for Meaning" and built it around the concept that individuals may change their focus from wanting external markers of success (money, prestige, titles) to desiring more internal meaning from their jobs. Any group with a core focus on creating meaning would incorporate existential principles.

Experiential Learning

Members enter groups with a variety of learning styles that may challenge the leader's ability to help each member make meaningful changes. Kolb's experiential learning theory (1984) has been successful in engaging different styles. This theory has two components: a four-stage learning cycle and four learning styles. The cycle consists of a concrete experience (CE), reflective observation (RO), abstract conceptualization (AC), and active experimentation (AE). In its most basic form, individuals must first take in information through some type of experience and then act upon that information through reflection and observation. These reflections lead to new ways of understanding, creating more options for actions (Kolb et al., 2014). While undergoing the four-stage cycle, individuals demonstrate a preference for some of the components. Diverging learners prefer feeling and watching (CE/RO), whereas assimilating learners have a preference for watching and thinking (AC/RO). Converging learners engage in doing and thinking (AC/AE), and accommodating learners prefer doing and feeling (CE/AE). Therefore, it is important for the group design to incorporate each of the four components in a psychoeducational group session. A topic can begin with some type of hands-on experience (CE), followed by time to reflect upon the experience (RO). This sequence can be followed by a theoretical model (AC) and acted upon by a practical application (AE).

Keune and Salter (2022) have researched how experiential learning moves students from learning content ("what") to understanding how to use information ("how"). This transition was found to improve individual outcomes. While there is debate about the effectiveness of the experiential learning model, Miller and Maellaro (2016) found that including collective group reflection increased the accuracy of what students learned. This model fits well with structured groups because activities often take place in smaller subgroups where members can apply new knowledge to problematic situations and share responses with each other. The use of dyads or triads ensures that each member will be an active participant in the activity. Research has also demonstrated that applying experiential learning to skill development has positive learning outcomes (Dewi et al., 2023; Meyer et al., 2021).

Structured groups are frequently designed to facilitate comprehension about a mental health issue and build skills to improve the situation. Designing a group around core experiential learning concepts can expedite this process. Besides providing valuable information about a topic, opportunities both for reflecting on how the issue impacts members and for forming ideas about how to approach the issue can lead to practicing behaviors that reduce the issue. Too often, issue-focused groups merely provide information without helping the members make meaningful change. For example, a stress management group might share definitions of stress and even teach some relaxation techniques. However, helping individuals examine faulty thinking and teaching skills to change stress-producing thoughts would better equip them to prevent future problems. The design process presented in this workbook can help the leader develop a comprehensive approach to true change.

One question that arises is the impact of cultural differences on learning style. Joy and Kolb (2009) conducted an international study examining how culture might impact learning style. They found that culture made a small but significant contribution to the preferred learning stages of AC over CE, with culture explaining 2% of the variance, gender explaining 1%, level of education explaining 2%, and job specialization explaining 3%. On the AE-RO dimension, age (2%) and specialization (1%) made significant contributions to AE over RO. Although culture does need to be considered, its impact on learning style is limited.

From Conceptualization to Implementation

Translating an innovative idea into a successful, structured group is no easy task. The idea for the group may have evolved from informally observing the needs of students, clients, or employees, or it may be a response to a formal needs assessment. In either case, the idea must be developed into a workable plan that addresses the concerns of individuals. The ideas must be translated into actionable steps for the individual to achieve meaningful change. Although increasing awareness of the problem or need is a necessary step to change, awareness alone is not enough to ensure that change will occur.

This book demonstrates a step-by-step guide for designing structured groups. Portions of this conceptual model were previously introduced in a presentation by Furr (myself) and Fulkerson (1982) and expanded upon in an article by Furr (2000). This third iteration substantially expands, updates, and applies that framework. Additionally, this volume provides practical examples and worksheets to guide leaders in their planning, design, and implementation of structured groups.

Although the content of the group will vary, the process of design remains constant. The design process is both creative and demanding. Because psychological interests and concerns can be viewed from a variety of theoretical perspectives, each idea can be transformed into many different structured groups. For example, a weight management group can be designed from a behavioral, Gestalt, or reality therapy perspective. Each group would take a different direction, with the behavioral approach emphasizing the use of reinforcement, a Gestalt approach concentrating on awareness of feelings connected with eating, and the reality approach addressing consequences and making choices. Although the goals of each group would be similar, the techniques utilized to achieve the goals would vary. With so many options to consider, the design of the group is limited only by the creativity of the designer.

It's important to be as thorough as possible when designing a group. Planning each component can be tedious and time-consuming, but these front-end efforts are beneficial long-term because the plan can be implemented repeatedly with many different groups. Designers often want to leave out "insignificant" details only to discover later that they cannot recall the intricacies of an exercise. Careful attention to each step in the design process results in a format that is easily reusable in the future. The original time investment is repaid each time the structured group is conducted.

A good benchmark to meet when creating a structured group manual is adding enough detail to the design that a trained counselor or similar professional could implement it without having to conduct extensive research before leading the group. In other words, the only element they need to succeed is the manual. A structured group manual must identify the group's goals and objectives, intended members, didactic content, experiential exercises, and processing questions and issues to address. The group leader may want to be flexible regarding how a particular exercise or lecture is implemented, but they should not need to make judgments about the purpose or intended content of a session. That should all be included in the manual.

The guiding elements when designing a group are the issues that the group seeks to mitigate and the theoretical perspective upon which it relies. With these two factors, the designer can craft a six-step procedure for the group. Part 2 details how to use theory to guide design. Once theory is determined, the design process can begin. Part 3 covers the first three steps of the design, which explore what the group is trying to achieve. These steps are (1) establishing a statement of purpose, (2) determining goals, and (3) setting objectives (Furr & Fulkerson, 1982; Furr, 2000). Part 4 covers the next three steps, which focus on how the group operates and achieves its goals. These steps are (4) selection of content, (5) designing exercises, and (6) evaluation.

Each step is followed by an example from a structured group I designed and led. Because the steps apply to a wide range of topics, leaders are encouraged to examine other examples of groups that are discussed in the literature. Each example is followed by an outline of how to create your own content for your group.

Structured groups provide counselors with an additional approach to support clients in developing or enhancing their skills to manage mental health issues. Research has shown favorable outcomes for clients who engage in this type of counseling experience. These groups can be designed for almost any client population over a variety of topics. This book focuses on how to design a dynamic experience for clients that will facilitate their development. By following the format presented here, leaders will be able to develop content, activities, and processing methods to create an effective and engaging group experience.

2

Theory to Practice

For many counselors, theory is an interesting set of hypotheses that explains elements of human behavior. However, when applying theory to actual clients, the relevance becomes less clear. Psychological theories typically answer questions about human nature. Different theories offer different approaches and answers to specific questions. When a client poses a question, a counselor can refer to several theoretical approaches and then decide which one better assists with the client's particular situation. This chapter covers common theories as applied to structured groups and concludes with a discussion about how to utilize a theoretical approach for topics commonly addressed in structured groups.

The Key Questions

In counseling, it can be challenging to find a connection between theory and action. Theoretical approaches often feel too abstract, too vague, to apply to a specific client and their challenges. For example, psychodynamic theory examines how unconscious drives influence personality and defines the roles of the id, ego, and superego (American Psychological Association [APA], n.d.). However, translating this theory into a treatment protocol may be difficult due to the need to discover how to uncover primal impulses that are manifested in daily behavior. In contrast, cognitive behavior theory (CBT) may present a more direct path to treatment because that approach involves counselors directly challenging irrational thoughts. When the counselor moves from examining the surface thoughts to core beliefs, the theory may become more complex. To make the theory more comprehensible, it is important to recognize that theories guide our approach to clients by offering answers to practical questions.

With the right approach, theory can be a useful tool when counseling individuals or groups. Before opening a textbook, it is important to understand that theory is a guide to answering questions about the client. Each question holds key information that assists in understanding how to facilitate change in a client. For a structured group to be effective, the leader must identify what information clients need for change to be initiated, as well as appropriate techniques for fostering that change. The group leader can choose an existing theory and build the group based on this theory. A group focused on building self-esteem could incorporate a humanistic theory wherein clients investigate who they are at their core and focus on unconditional acceptance of self. This group could also take a cognitive approach and focus on identifying, challenging, and changing negative thoughts about themselves. Both theories address valuable aspects of a person, and it is the leader's responsibility to choose the theory they believe best fits the topic of the group.

Although counselors are familiar with the major theories used in the field, group leaders can also create a "theory" of change for the topic of their structured group. Using this approach, the group leader takes their knowledge about the group topic and blends several theories to best address the needs of the members. For example, a group about building self-esteem may focus on how thoughts, emotions, and behaviors interact to maintain a client's negative view of self and incorporate these three perspectives into their group. To make this determination, the leader should examine the group's topic by asking a series of questions. The leader needs to be aware of their understanding of how the problem developed for their group topic and how they believe change occurs. A good theory would address each of these questions and provide a roadmap for the direction of the group. Counselors who are designing a structured group must ask themselves each of these questions prior to beginning their group design. Their answers guide the design process.

What Is the Nature of People?

One of the first assumptions to examine in a theory is its basic view of the nature of people. Does the theory foster the view that people are born basically good? Or is the assumption made that people must fight against innate forces and impulses that are destructive? Perhaps the theory is based on the idea that people are neither good nor are they prone to harmful actions. Instead, the view may be that behavior is learned and dependent on the environment in which the person lives. When applied to structured groups, each of these views would require a different approach to group design. For example, a theory such as Rogerian, or client-centered, would focus on the person's innate ability to discover within the self the capacity for change and to reduce the incongruence between self-concept and ideal self-concept (APA, n.d.). Consequently, a structured group would assist members in identifying these discrepancies and provide support for making appropriate changes. In contrast, a structured group based on CBT would assume that people are neither inherently good nor bad but that they rather learn from their environment. They can change inappropriate thoughts and behaviors if given the proper instruction and practice. That type of group would be more focused on teaching and practice of skills than on self-examination.

Structured Group Example Answer

In a group focused on stress management, the assumption is made that stress is a natural response to perceived threats. While there are individual variations in each person's genetic makeup, other factors such as life experiences and environmental factors also contribute to one's stress response. A psychoeducational group focused on stress management would be built on the premise that people can learn constructive ways to respond to stressful situations.

What Is Healthy Development?

Before a counselor can assist a person in changing unhealthy patterns, it is important to understand how a person develops what would be considered "normal" or healthy characteristics. A counselor's assumptions about human nature guide the direction they take with their clients. Their theory about human nature explains if development occurs through learning, the resolution of a developmental stage or the fulfillment of a need or instinct. To understand what needs to happen within the group, the target outcome must be clearly established. This process is dependent upon establishing the beliefs, thoughts, feelings, and behaviors considered to be healthy. If the leader can determine what the ideal outcome will be, then goals can be established to obtain the desired changes. Once again, the theory selected will outline what is considered healthy development. For example, client-centered theory views healthy development as congruence, whereas cognitive theory sees it as having rational thoughts about perceived threats.

Structured Group Example Answer

From a cognitive behavior point of view, the client needs to develop skills to tackle difficult situations and believe in their own capability to confront adversity to manage stress. Rather than seeing a threat as an impossible barrier and thus inflating its power, a CBT approach breaks down the components of a threat into manageable tasks and strategies to address the task.

How Does Development Go Awry?

After healthy development is defined within a theoretical foundation, leaders should identify disruptions in development. Was the individual reinforced for inappropriate behaviors? Client development can go awry in childhood if the adults in their life neglect to meet the child's needs. That neglect, in turn, can block the client's successful negotiation of crucial life stages. From a Gestalt perspective, the client may be unaware of emotions and block them from awareness, leaving unresolved needs. Regardless of the theoretical orientation selected, in order to successfully enact change in group members, a leader must identify how, in their own view, healthy development occurs and what interferes with healthy development. Structured group topics tend to be specific, such as managing stress or building self-esteem. The first step in determining the group content is for the leader to determine how they believe a person builds a positive sense of self. If the group is geared toward building positive communication skills, the leader should identify how that can occur naturally. Understanding healthy development is key to developing positive outcome goals for the group.

Structured Group Example Answer

Someone who attends a stress management group may have encountered several challenges in dealing with stress. Perhaps their family members viewed any challenge as a potential threat and, when faced with a difficult situation, succumbed to extreme stress. That could result in the group member developing a fear of new situations. Homes in which perfection is expected may create a mindset that any imperfection is a failure, thus laying the groundwork for negative self-evaluation. When a person experiences actual failure, how they process it (or fail to process it) can lead to negative cognitions about future challenges. Rather than seeing failure as an opportunity to grow and learn, the person feels devalued and defeated. Much of the process of dealing with difficult situations is learned early in life, but can be modified by learning new perspectives.

How Does Change Occur?

Every psychological theory makes assumptions about how people change. This issue comprises the core of the structured group. The group design is dependent upon the assumptions made about how change can be facilitated. Does change occur through gaining new skills and knowledge? How important is insight to the change process? What role is played by significant others in promoting change? Does the environment need to be altered for change to be lasting? The leader must be aware of the type of change the group is proposing to facilitate. Both content and process are derived from the assumptions about change and are dependent on the implementation of sound theoretical concepts. Developing self-esteem is one topic that would be approached differently depending upon which theory is selected for the design. If a cognitive behavior approach is selected, the leader would concentrate on changing maladaptive thoughts. However, if the leader chooses to use a client-centered approach, they would focus on member insight about unconditional acceptance of self.

Structured Group Example Answer

Taking a cognitive behavior approach to stress management, the group would help members identify messages and experiences they have encountered in dealing with previous threats. Negative messages would be challenged and modified. The body's response to negative thinking would also be examined, knowing that negative thoughts can influence physical response. Learning to reduce physiological symptoms while increasing productive thinking can empower members to change how they respond in stressful situations.

Next Steps

In answering the four key questions, the leader may find that one theory does not encompass all aspects of the group topic. Each theory tends to draw from one aspect of development: cognitive, affective, or behavioral. However, people are complex and may need to address multiple channels of change. Consequently, the leader may want to evolve their personal theoretical approach to the topic when designing a group. After the group topic is selected, the next step is to ask the key questions in relation to the topic. For example, in designing a group to improve self-esteem, the leader needs to ask what assumptions group members are making about the nature of people and self-esteem. Are people born with a good sense of self, or are they born with a negative sense of worth that must be overcome? Perhaps individuals are born without a specific sense of worth and learn this from their interactions in the environment. When the leader determines the answer to this question, they then ask how a healthy sense of self develops, as well as what prevents a healthy self from developing. In answering these two questions, the leader will most likely identify both internal and external factors that impact development.

At times, the answers to what leads to healthy development will be opposite to the answers to how development goes awry. If an environment filled with unconditional acceptance leads to healthy development, then an environment that only has conditional acceptance will create unhealthy development. From a different theoretical perspective, the leader may observe that self-esteem is high in children who receive positive feedback tied to positive efforts and achievements, but low in children who only receive criticism regardless of effort and achievement. In turn, children who have received positive affirmations may be better able to engage in positive self-talk than children who only hear criticisms. Each of these observations provides a block to build a theoretical structure about self-esteem that includes cognitions, affect, and behavior. The leader then would take this information and ask, "How does change in self-esteem occur?" The answer would include elements from all three aspects of self-esteem: self-talk, internalized feelings about self, and behaviors that reflect self-talk and feelings.

Armed with a newly developed perspective on the group topic, the leader is now equipped to begin outlining the parameters of the group content. When the leader comprehends the developmental process in relation to the group topic, they can draw from a variety of existing theories to address the various aspects of human development. People are complex in terms of how they learn and grow. Few theories cover all these aspects, so evolving a blended perspective specific to the group topic will enhance the group's ability to be effective in creating lasting change for the group members. The following activity outlines how to apply theory to your chosen group topic.

Worksheet: Developing Your Theoretical Perspective

1. What is the central focus of your group? (What will be the main topic that attracts people to the group?)

2. What is the nature of people? (Are people shaped by their biology, driven by emotions, or influenced by their thoughts?)

3. What is healthy development? (How does an individual naturally develop the characteristic that is the focus of the group?)

4. How does development go awry? (What interferes with an individual developing this characteristic?)

5. How does change occur? (What is your belief about how clients change? Is it through learning new behaviors, expression of emotions, or changing irrational thoughts?)

3

Conceptualizing the Group
Purpose, Goals, and Objectives

Structured groups consist of more than a set of activities that the leader hopes will increase the members' awareness and knowledge. An effective structured group is grounded in theory and research that supports the application of that theory. Once the theory is examined, a sense of purpose evolves that guides the development of goals and objectives. These three aspects together produce a foundation that supports an effective and efficient use of the members' time and energy. One of the greatest errors group leaders make is to choose a couple of activities without connecting the activities to the group's theoretical foundation. Even if the activities are exciting and produce some insight, lasting change will not occur if they are not embedded in the larger purpose of the group. Originally presented by Furr (myself) and Fulkerson (1982), expanded upon by Furr (2000), and substantially updated and applied in this volume, these steps are a model for designing a structured group. The three steps described in this section serve to produce a strong foundation for the content and activities of the structured group. These steps are critical for later design of group activities with the idea that creating a clear focus will lead to the development of group content that builds sequentially to create a positive outcome for members. Part 3 describes the first three steps of the model. They allow leaders to produce a strong foundation for the content and activities of the structured group. These steps are critical to accomplish before moving on to the design of group activities in later steps (Part 4). Creating a clear focus leads to the development of group content that builds sequentially and creates a positive outcome for members.

Step 1: Statement of Purpose

After the leader has conceived an idea for a group, they must determine the purpose of the group (Furr & Fulkerson, 1982; Furr, 2000). If the purpose is unclear, the group will flounder from a lack of direction. Often, the answer to the question of purpose seems quite simple. One only has to look at the title of the proposed group to determine its reason for existing. The purpose of an assertion training group is to teach people to be assertive, right? Maybe, but a good leader goes beyond the initial concept when determining the purpose. Is it an assertion group to teach behavior, make people aware of their rights, or explore unexpressed anger? Is the group open to anyone or is it designed for a special population, such as nurses? The purpose needs to be stated explicitly. Without a clearly delineated direction, the leader can lose focus and orientation. When the purpose is not clearly stated, the consumer or member may develop unrealistic expectations and be disappointed with the outcome. The purpose guides the development of goals and content as well as facilitates congruency between the expectations of leaders and members.

After determining the general topic, the leader must decide how they view the topic theoretically (Furr & Fulkerson, 1982; Furr, 2000). This process is described in Part 2. All groups expect some type of change to occur in the group members. This change may be in awareness, knowledge, insight, cognitions, or behavior. Each leader makes assumptions about the type of change expected. Awareness of these assumptions is necessary before goals and content can be determined. Assumptions may be related to a particular theory, such as Gestalt, cognitive behavior theory (CBT), or existential. In other instances, the assumptions may integrate ideas from several theories as they relate to the particular focus of the group. For example, self-esteem may initially be defined from a client-centered view of unconditional acceptance of self. After a few sessions utilizing that approach, the leader may shift to a CBT approach that focuses on changing negative, esteem-damaging messages. Regardless of the theoretical orientation, the leader needs to acknowledge these assumptions before designing content.

After the topic and theoretical approach have been determined, additional parameters need to be established. The leader must first know the limitations of the group. In general, structured groups are unable to promote environmental or system changes. The leader may want to consider whether individual changes will be supported by the individual's primary environments. If these environments ignore or even punish the change, then the change will disappear. For example, a school district may want its students to become more assertive in dealing with peer pressure, but as students develop these skills, they may also become more assertive with teachers or parents, which could lead to conflict. The environment needs to be supportive of the changes proposed in the structured group, or the group needs to address how their changes will affect their environment.

Structured groups have little impact on significant others unless the group is specifically designed to include people such as parents, spouses, and partners. The leader must determine the appropriate scope of the group and the importance of including influential people in the group process. If the group fosters individual change that is dependent upon support from outside relationships, the group may not be successful unless it includes every person involved in the change process. Consequently, the leader needs to carefully construct the purpose of the group to only include those elements of change that can be handled within the group context. If significant others are crucial to the change process, then the group design should incorporate methods of securing that support. For example, a group designed to assist children in coping with divorce might include a supplementary parent session on ways to support children during this transition by teaching parents not to involve children in adult decisions. When it is not feasible to include significant others, the leader needs to establish clarity about the purpose and limits of the group. Structured groups that focus on changing the individual through learning and insight can be a powerful instrument of change as long as the purpose remains clear.

A group's statement of purpose should also include the age range, genders, and cultural backgrounds of the members. Because developmental issues are pertinent to the theoretical assumptions of the group, age must be a consideration in the design. Awareness of the stages of child, adolescent, and adult development can strengthen the effectiveness of the group. Areas of cognitive development (e.g., Piaget; Perry), moral development (e.g., Kohlberg), emotional development (e.g., Erikson), and stages of life development (e.g., Levinson; Sheehy) need to be examined. A group aimed at inappropriate developmental stages will lessen the chances of success.

Gender and cultural factors are additional areas of consideration. Topics may need different emphases depending on the gender or cultural background of members. In his seminal work on teaching assertiveness to racial minorities, Cheek (1976) stated that "authors on assertiveness have not sufficiently considered the social conditions in which blacks live—and have lived. That blind spot in many ways alters or changes the manner that assertiveness is applied" (p. 11). This point illustrates the importance of understanding the population for which the group is designed. Although social conditions may have changed in the years post-publication, it is important to consider the cultural factors that may influence how the group topic is perceived by different populations. A structured group needs to accommodate these different perspectives so that members can maximize their ability to grow from the experience.

In determining whether a group is appropriate for a potential member, the leader needs to examine the person's previous group experience. If the structured group is designed as one module in a series of groups or for an existing group where members know each other, the issues surrounding cohesion and trust will differ from the issues found when group members have no common history. If there is no previously established bond, the group will need to budget time for building group cohesion. If there is a history among group members, the group will need to be designed to minimize any disruptive elements from the past.

Group members may or may not have prior experience in psychologically oriented groups. If any members have participated in therapy or encounter groups, their expectations of a structured group may be unrealistic. Others without group experience may have distorted or inaccurate views of the group process. They may not comprehend the commitment the member must make to the change process and may expect the leader to do all the work. Although it may be difficult to determine group experience before designing a group, careful attention must be given to educating members about the structured group process. This issue can be addressed either in the instructions in the group manual, in the overview presented to group members in the screening process, or in the first session.

Ask Yourself

To complete Step 1, leaders must answer the following questions:

1. What is the purpose of the group's existence?

2. For whom is the group designed (age, gender, cultural background, group experience, primary, secondary, or tertiary prevention)

3. What is the overarching focus of psychosocial change addressed in the group?

4. How does theory guide the group design (see Part 2)? (How do the following elements guide the group design?)

   a. What is the nature of people?

   b. How does normal development occur?

   c. How does development go awry?

   d. How does change take place?

EXAMPLE

Building Self-Esteem Group: Statement of Purpose

The group, Building Self-Esteem, is designed for undergraduate students who desire to develop more positive feelings about themselves. Self-esteem is the ability to understand one's own strengths and limitations, and to accept and value oneself unconditionally. The group design is based on the assumption that self-esteem is learned through interactions with others and with the environment. People are not born with positive or negative self-esteem, but with the capacity to develop in either direction.

Children learn to value themselves through receiving positive messages from significant others and eventually internalize these messages and apply them to their own actions. Self-esteem also develops when the child can direct their behavior in ways that result in achievement and success. Self-esteem comes both from being valued unconditionally and from one's sense of accomplishment. Development can go awry in several ways. If the child is ignored or receives constant criticism from the significant others in their life, they may not feel they are valued. This situation can lead to the child internalizing a negative view of self. Another situation that leads to poor self-esteem is when the child receives conditional acceptance. The child is only accepted when they have done something well. The child then becomes dependent upon external praise to feel good about self rather than accepting their unconditional value as a person. Sometimes, people are not given the opportunity to develop their talents and consequently do not believe they are capable of success. They may develop a mindset of failure and personal worthlessness. Cultural standards may also hinder the development of self-esteem. A child may be taught that acknowledging one's good qualities is equivalent to bragging. The cultural group may believe that people are inherently bad and do not have the right to feel good about themselves. Another issue may come from a child receiving too much praise regardless of level of performance. Healthy self-esteem comes from valuing one's efforts in those areas where they have control (Mueller & Dweck, 1998).

Whatever the reason behind the development of a negative self-image, adults maintain these feelings about self through their own beliefs and cognitions. Change, therefore, occurs by modifying the belief system and the ensuing cognitions and self-talk. Change can also be facilitated by adjusting self-defeating behaviors and engaging in rewarding behaviors. The individual needs to learn that they can provide unconditional acceptance of the self, as well as change behaviors to be more success-oriented.

The purpose of this group is to provide members with the knowledge and skills to recognize the role negative cognitions play in how they evaluate themselves and then to develop skills to reduce negative thoughts and replace them with a more positive view of self that leads to unconditional acceptance. Through increased knowledge supported by group activities, members will develop the ability to become more supportive of themselves and build a stronger sense of self-efficacy.

Step 2: Establishing Goals

Now that the group has a definition of purpose, the leader needs to establish goals that demonstrate what the group members can achieve in the group. How will the individual members be different when the group is completed? Goals can be conceptualized as the compass that guides the direction of how members will change. Changes can occur on cognitive, behavioral, emotional, physical, and existential levels (Furr & Fulkerson, 1982; Furr, 2000). The leader needs to specify the type(s) of change expected as a result of participating in the group. The goals for change will be derived from the theoretical perspective selected in the statement of purpose. If the theory specifies that change occurs through learning and rehearsing new behaviors, the goals will be more behavioral than if the theory is based on insight. Theories that emphasize affective approaches to change will have goals focused on the emotional domain. Goals based on insight and affect are not as easily evaluated as goals based on cognitive and behavior change, but these goals still can provide the group members with explicit direction regarding ways to recognize and express emotions, even though the group will not focus on deep expression of feelings during sessions.

Clearly written goals allow members to evaluate the group in terms of personal needs. In some cases, a member may be specifically interested in changing a behavior, whereas another may want to gain an understanding of the motivation behind a behavior. Another may want to express emotions caused by a particular issue that may have been suppressed or ignored. The structured group format has the flexibility to accommodate each of these approaches, but it may not be appropriate to attempt to accomplish all these goals in one group. The leader may have to choose which approach the group will emphasize and clearly communicate what the group plans to do to accomplish it. Because of the brief nature of structured groups, deeper exploration of emotions may not be possible. In this case, a therapeutic group may be more appropriate. Knowing what members desire from the group is crucial. Without that knowledge, members will become disenchanted with the process because their needs are not being addressed. Clearly defining the parameters of a group will help members determine if the structured group format is a good fit for them.

Writing Goals

A goal indicates what can be attained through participation in the group. Implicit to any goal is the idea that the individual is willing to take the action necessary to achieve the goal. This idea is particularly relevant to structured groups. Members must be committed to investing energy in the process by participating in the activities, absorbing the information presented, and self-disclosing as appropriate. The leader needs to communicate to members the importance of committing to the group's goals. Group participation cannot give an individual a new characteristic or quality, but can only provide a framework for the person to change through their own efforts.

For goals to be meaningful, several major criteria must be met (Furr & Fulkerson, 1982; Furr, 2000). A useful method for determining an effective goal is one that follows a variation of the SMART (specific, measurable/meaningful, achievable, relevant/reasonable/rewarding, and time-bound/trackable) format. The goal should be specific, clear, and well-defined. The goal includes who will be involved, what will be accomplished, and how it will take place. Goals need to be clearly defined for members to determine if the goals are consistent with their personal value systems. Rather than a goal that states that members will improve self-esteem, a specific goal would focus on increasing positive self-statements through identifying and modifying negative self-talk. If goals are too general, they may expect the group to eradicate all their problems. It is important that members recognize the group has limitations in its scope.

A second criterion for goal setting is that the goal be measurable (Furr & Fulkerson, 1982; Furr, 2000). Vague goals such as becoming a better person may sound impressive, but are difficult to evaluate in terms of success. How will members know when they have achieved what the group has to offer? When goals are defined in terms of behaviors, members will have a clear conception of possible outcomes. It may not be possible to define all goals in terms of behavior; therefore, outcomes based on cognitions and affect may become necessary as well.

Not only should goals be measurable, but goals also need to be meaningful (Furr & Fulkerson, 1982; Furr, 2000). If a group is to be effective, members must believe that the experience will add something important to their lives. In a group directed toward helping individuals reassess and modify their values, members need to see the benefits of making those changes for the group to be successful. Often, a group focuses on a specific population because the behaviors of and values held by that population are widely considered inappropriate. For example, there are many groups designed to help adolescents say no to drugs or to avoid teenage pregnancy. Unfortunately, these groups may fail if they only address the values and beliefs underpinning the behaviors of drug use or teenage pregnancy, not the behaviors themselves. Helping members make meaning of the desired change is essential to group success. If a group addresses topics involving personal values, the leader needs to be aware of how these values impact the topic. When a particular cultural, social, or religious value conflicts with the philosophical assumptions of the group, the leader needs to recognize the potential discrepancy. However, in most cases, the group design can include a section on values and will help individuals resolve their own conflicts. Even when the goal is behavioral change, it is important for values to be examined because a behavior is difficult to maintain unless it is consistent with a member's values.

A goal must be achievable. Do the members have the resources necessary to reach the group's goals? These resources include abilities, attitudes, and skills. A goal may be admirable, but members may enter the group deficient in the basic skills needed to benefit from the group. Consequently, the leader would need to expand the goals so that they include learning basic skills that can be used later in the group. The leader must be attuned to the level of functioning of joining members or else risk creating an experience of failure for the members (Furr & Fulkerson, 1982; Furr, 2000). Consider a group on parenting. Most conventional parenting groups are organized based on the assumption that parents have high reading abilities, as well as the financial resources to do activities with their children. However, one specific group, led by one of my students, was comprised of members who were participating in a program to help them gain employment. The parents were on public financial assistance and were in danger of losing their children due to neglect. Although they cared deeply for their children and their motivation to change was high, their ability to utilize some of the more common parenting materials was limited. The group's leader adjusted her group to reduce the amount of reading, included more visual aids, and added more modeling and hands-on practice sessions. She was able to enhance the members' parenting skills within the parameters of their current abilities and resources.

Goals must also be relevant. Members need to believe that the goals are appropriate for their needs. A goal is usually relevant if the member truly believes that achieving this goal will make a difference in their life. Does the result of achieving the goal matter to them? Members need to understand that the goals will be challenging but that they have a high probability of responding to the challenge successfully with a positive outcome in their lives. When goals are relevant, achieving them directly contributes to a sense of success, encouraging the member to continue to grow.

In addition to being relevant, a goal must also be reasonable (Furr & Fulkerson, 1982; Furr, 2000). Members need to believe that they are reasonably able to achieve the goal and that it is meeting a specific need. The member should be able to look at the goal and think, "I believe I can do that." If the goals seem unreasonable, people will either avoid participating for fear of failure or will develop unrealistic expectations of what the group will do for them. When expectations go unmet, feelings of doubt and disappointment can develop. Members need to see that the goals will be challenging but that they have a high probability of responding to the challenge successfully.

Goals also need to be viewed by members as potentially rewarding. Nothing sustains success like rewards. If a member can experience the benefits of working toward change, that member is more likely to continue to pursue the goal. From the perspective of reality therapy (American Psychological Association, n.d.), people will engage in actions that help them fulfill their needs, including developing a sense of self-worth and achievement. Goals that are written in a way that demonstrates the benefits of pursuing specific actions will increase the motivation of members to take risks in the group.

Finally, goals must be time-bound and trackable (Furr & Fulkerson, 1982; Furr, 2000). The leader must distinguish between short-range and long-range goals. Members enter a structured group with a lifetime accumulation of behaviors, beliefs, values, and emotions. It is naïve to think that a six- or eight-session structured group is going to completely alter negative patterns. But it is possible to equip members with the tools for future change. By breaking change into smaller units that can be achieved in specified time frames, members can track each step in the change process. The best way to view the structured group is as a springboard for motivating the individual to seek further growth. The group is an excellent method for allowing the member to experience change in a safe environment. Once this experience has occurred, the person will be prepared to continue the path to change.

Goals should be written in the active voice, using verbs that indicate what will happen in the group. It may be helpful to begin the goal with the word "to" followed by an action verb. This language indicates that members are expected to be active participants in their learning. Not only are they expected to participate in the group activities, but there is also an expectation that they apply these lessons to their lives outside of the group. Unless the goals are clearly stated in terms of what will occur during the time of the group, members may believe that they will be dramatically different after the group experience. They need to be aware that they may gain knowledge, insight, and some new behaviors through the group, but that these gains are only the beginning. The group's short-range goals can be translated into long-range goals that continue after the group is completed. It is the leader's responsibility to differentiate between short-range and long-range goals and to demonstrate how these goals can be integrated. If a group is designed well, the short-range goals will provide successive steps that enable the member to reach larger goals.

Ask Yourself

To complete Step 2, leaders must answer the following questions:

1. How will members be different when the group is completed?
2. In what area(s) will the individual be different?
   a. cognitive,
   b. behaviors,
   c. emotions,
   d. insights, or
   e. physical?
3. Are the goals reasonable and measurable?
4. How do members' values align with these goals?
5. What are the short-range versus long-range goals?

EXAMPLE

Building Self-Esteem Group: Establishing Goals

The following goals were established for the group, Building Self-Esteem, to be achieved by the group's completion.

1. To foster an understanding of the relationship between self-talk and self-esteem and to learn to modify inappropriate self-talk.

2. To increase awareness of how emotions relate to self-talk, with special emphasis on the ways people use self-talk to cancel out positive feelings.

3. To develop an understanding of how beliefs, self-talk, and feelings can influence behavior and to instigate changes that lead to productive behaviors.

4. To facilitate clarification of personal values and recognize the importance of living consistently with personal values.

5. To examine how both internal and external "put-downs" affect self-esteem and to establish responses to address inappropriate criticism.

Step 3: Setting Objectives

Although goals give a general direction for the group, more specific steps within those goals need to be defined. Objectives provide the mechanism for connecting session content with goals (Furr & Fulkerson, 1982; Furr, 2000). Whereas goals are the compass pointing the group in the right direction, objectives are the roadmap that shows a step-by-step way to reach the goal. Objectives specify the steps necessary for reaching the group goals. Each goal should be followed by objectives that will enable the members to achieve the goal. After goals are established, the leader must decide how best to achieve the goals. The leader must translate the theoretical basis for that group into a practical application of content and group process. Applying theory to practice is not always easy, but without this step, the group will not flow in a logical sequence.

In setting objectives, the leader makes assumptions about the way a particular psychological concept evolves. While psychological theories such as Gestalt or Rogerian discuss personal development in global terms, the leader must use the designated theory to formulate specific hypotheses about the topic under study before objectives can be set. The leader needs to ask what the theory says about how this specific behavior, characteristic, or state develops, and what steps one can take to gain this quality. In short, the leader must evolve their theory of development as it applies to the topic of the group. For example, the group topic may be time management that the leader has decided to approach from a behavioral viewpoint. The leader would need to ask what primary behaviors create roadblocks to effective time management and what steps can be taken to remedy this problem. The leader would make assumptions (based on current research) about the development of healthy and unhealthy time management behaviors and concentrate on what behavioral changes members would need to make. However, the leader may view time management issues as a more existential issue based on how choices revolve around one's personal values. The group approach would then focus on identifying what is important to the individual and examining how these values affect choices made about the use of one's time.

Identifying the specific steps necessary for change is a crucial element in designing a structured group (Furr & Fulkerson, 1982; Furr, 2000). The objectives become the bridge between theory and practice. Whereas the goals are derived from the theory, the objectives put the theory in motion. The session-by-session content of the group is derived directly from the objectives. Consequently, objectives must be written in a specific manner. Objectives indicate what should happen for the goal to be met. Thus, objectives provide an outline for the content. When the objectives are specified, the leader can choose from many creative approaches to meet the objectives. Whereas goals are written in more global terms beginning with "to," objectives define how this action will take place and often use the language "members will" to indicate steps the members will take. To accomplish a goal, a group needs multiple objectives, usually between three and five. If more than five objectives are needed, the goal may be too broad and may need to be divided into two separate goals.

Often, the content of a group session will center around one of the objectives. For example, the leader may hypothesize that a low self-image is maintained by the critical messages an individual gives self. In this case, one or more sessions may be designed around the issue of self-talk and changing cognitions. The leader would then combine information and activities in a way that would impact the thoughts and internal messages of the members. The objectives serve the purpose of connecting the goals with the content of the group and need to contain specific terminology about the dimension of change being addressed to serve as a guide for the sessions.

Objectives make assumptions about the various dimensions where individual change occurs. Change is possible on multiple dimensions, and successful groups attempt to reach people on more than one level (Furr, 2000). Learning is more meaningful and more impactful when the individual is reached through several dimensions. The most obvious channel for change is the behavioral dimension. Early structured groups were oriented almost exclusively toward modifying people's behavior. Many modern groups still incorporate behavior change principles, although these techniques may be integrated with other approaches. Groups that promise behavior change may rely heavily on role-playing and operant-conditioning procedures such as positive reinforcement and response consequences (Curtis, 2014). In cases concerned with individuals who need to learn basic social skills or to eliminate inappropriate social behavior, a focus on the behavioral dimension has been beneficial.

A corollary to the behavioral level is the cognitive dimension (Beck, 2005). Practitioners have recognized that behaviors do not occur in a vacuum. At times, problems occur because an individual does not have the information necessary to change inappropriate behavior. The person would behave differently if only they knew alternative responses. One function of the structured group is to teach members what they need to know to initiate personal change. Leaders of structured groups make the assumption that there are psychological principles that can be taught directly to individuals and that, through applying these principles, individuals can achieve change. An essential part of any structured group is conveying information to the members that leads them to develop a different perspective on their issues. Clients have frequently reported that counseling has helped them have a different perspective on their issues (Beck, 2005). By changing thinking patterns, clients can respond differently to life's challenges.

Another aspect of the cognitive dimension deals with the individual's value and belief systems. A major thrust of cognitive theory is examining destructive or irrational beliefs a person may hold (Ellis, 1997). When a person incorporates a belief system into their life that is based on inaccurate or negative content, this belief system may create feelings of anxiety, worry, or depression. Helping members identify, challenge, and reject their irrational beliefs can increase positive feelings about themselves as well as facilitate behavior change. However, strongly held beliefs or principles can undermine even the best behavior change program. Because an individual's beliefs are a guiding force in their life, these beliefs must be examined, challenged, and possibly changed. Lasting change can only be accomplished when values and beliefs support the change.

A third dimension of change is the affective or emotional level. After the cognitive and behavioral levels are addressed, it becomes apparent that these levels are not isolated from emotions. The strength of a belief is grounded in the emotional associations of that belief. Even though a belief may be illogical, the emotions connected to that belief may keep it alive. To deal with a person's belief system also entails focusing on emotions. Feelings are often the "warning bell" that something is amiss. Clients do not tend to seek counseling for their thoughts (unless it was related to some type of psychosis or obsessive thinking)—they seek it because of their disruptive *feelings*. To be helpful, counselors need to recognize the interconnections of thoughts and feelings.

Emotions have largely been treated as the province of the therapy group and have not been viewed as a legitimate aspect of structured groups. Although structured groups do not delve into the depths of the psyche, leaders do need to recognize when to include an emotional focus. Even a factual topic such as time management can evoke an emotional response from an individual who struggles with it. A member who procrastinates may fear failure or may feel too inadequate to complete the task. Unless these emotional states are addressed, the member will not be able to successfully implement behavior change. Too frequently, structured groups have ignored this area, leaving members with knowledge but no lasting impact. Motivation comes from an emotional desire to change, not from knowledge about how to change. Consequently, the effective structured group focuses on the total person and includes behaviors, thoughts, and feelings as well as understanding the interplay among them.

Groups will vary in their emphasis on emotions. Some groups will concentrate on integrating these first three levels (cognitions, behaviors, and emotions), whereas other groups may focus exclusively on emotions. If the group topic is dependent upon an exploration of affective issues, the leader needs to set limits with the group members, or the group may evolve into a therapy group. Emotional issues can be addressed in a structured format if the leader is clear about the boundaries of each exercise. The group leader must be prepared to bring discussions to a close and allow adequate time for processing. The leader needs to anticipate the impact of the various group activities and only include those that can be conducted within the limitations of the group. Addressing emotional content within the structured group format is probably the most difficult area to design because individual responses are less predictable. Therefore, groups that focus only on emotions may demand more skilled leadership and may take more time.

The physical level is the fourth dimension of focus (Furr, 2000). Certain areas, such as stress management and weight management, are directly linked to one's physical self. Awareness of one's body and its physical sensations can aid a person in developing a holistic view of self. Increasing knowledge of the physical self may be essential to making changes in how the member treats their body. For some individuals, body awareness can be key to reaching the emotional level. Groups designed for persons with eating disorders or for women who have been sexually abused may draw heavily from experiential activities that involve body awareness. Although the physical aspect is not frequently incorporated into structured groups, the leader should be aware of those instances when this focus could provide an added dimension to the group.

The final dimension of focus is existential (Furr, 2000). Trying to define meaning in life is an integral task. Groups focusing on death and dying are a primary example of the need to include existential issues. These issues center on creating meaning in life through making choices in areas where choice is possible and finding meaning in areas where it is not. Structured exercises can be designed to help the individual understand choice and to actualize their potential through these choices. Whenever the group content assists an individual in re-examining life choices and meaning, the existential dimension is tapped.

In setting objectives, it is important to examine both the steps necessary for goal attainment and the dimensions on which the individual can be impacted. Content will evolve in a natural sequence if the objectives are based on an understanding of how people change. The leader must recognize that not every objective will be addressed in every session. Frequently, a single objective will be the focus of an entire session. However, each objective should be sequenced so that it leads logically to the next. Proper sequencing helps ensure that the group has a natural progression, with one level of learning providing support for the next level (Furr, 2000). The leader needs to determine whether it is best to sequence from cognitions to emotions to behaviors or whether the opposite sequencing is more logical. Each objective provides a small step in the change process. Often, there is a need for members to have a grasp of the concepts being introduced, so the leader may need to start with early content with definitions. Then, other concepts can be built upon this knowledge. Complex behaviors can be broken down into small steps, with each subsequent step adding to the total behavior. The roles of cognitions, feelings, and behaviors can be integrated through this process until the target goal is achieved.

Finally, group members need to be involved on multiple levels. Knowledge gained through several channels is more effective and enduring than when only one dimension is addressed. Human interactions and insights are a complex mixture of several dimensions. Well-written objectives will direct the leader to consider the multiple facets of the individual when choosing content that leads to achieving goals.

Ask Yourself

To complete Step 3, leaders must answer the following questions:

1. How does this skill/characteristic/insight develop naturally?
2. What steps are necessary for an individual to gain this skill/characteristic/insight?
3. What dimension(s) of the individual will be addressed through the group (behavioral, cognitive, emotional, physical, and existential)?

EXAMPLE

Building Self-Esteem Group: Setting Objectives

The following objectives were derived from Goal 1 (to develop an understanding of the relationship between self-talk and self-esteem and to learn to modify inappropriate self-talk):

1. Members will develop an understanding of the definition of self-talk.
2. Members will be able to differentiate between positive, negative, and coping self-talk.
3. Members will learn to recognize the relationship between self-esteem and self-talk and determine how self-talk affects their own self-esteem.
4. Members will develop skills to modify negative self-talk by incorporating positive or coping self-talk.
5. Members will learn to evaluate the impact of engaging in more constructive self-talk.

Step 1 Worksheet: Writing a Statement of Purpose

1. Who is the group for (age, gender, orientation, cultural background)?

2. What is the specific focus of the group? What will be the topic of the group? What are the psychosocial issues to be addressed in the group?

3. What will be the focus of change in the group (cognitive, behavioral, affective)?

Step 2 Worksheet: Establishing Goals

1. What is the first step in change for this topic? (It may revolve around having definitions that clarify the terms being used.)

2. What are the dimensions of change that need to occur (cognitive, behavioral, emotional, insight, or physical)?

3. After an understanding of the topic is established, what type of change needs to take place first as a way of building a foundation?

4. What is the next level of change that needs to occur? (This question can be repeated until multiple levels of change are established.)

Step 3 Worksheet: Setting Objectives

1. Considering your group topic, what dimensions (behavioral, cognitive, emotional, physical, and existential) need to be addressed?

2. From the list of dimensions you selected in the prior step, determine which one is foundational for beginning the change process. In other words, select the dimension that must be addressed first.

3. Within this dimension, determine where the change process begins? (What is the most basic knowledge, skill, or insight needed to begin the change process?)

4. Determine each subsequent step needed to achieve the overall goal.

5. When the path to goal achievement is determined, identify the next goal to examine and follow the same process in breaking the goal into achievable objectives. Continue this process until all goals are delineated by their objectives.

Designing the Group
Selection of Content, Designing Exercises, and Evaluation

The preliminary work of determining the purpose, goals, and objectives (Steps 1–3) provides the foundation for Steps 4–6 (Furr, 2000). The work intensifies in the second half of the framework, when leaders plan the content of the group sessions. However, if leaders carefully and thoughtfully follow the first three steps, the group content will evolve in a natural and logical fashion. Unfortunately, many leaders begin their group designs by selecting content without previously establishing goals and objectives. Closely following each step of the framework mitigates that risk and prepares leaders to structure content in a way that facilitates lasting change for members.

Step 4: Selection of Content

It is common for leaders to build a foundation for their groups based on a favorite exercise, around which they design a session. Unfortunately, organizing groups in such a manner leads to disjointed and out-of-sequence concepts, rendering sessions ineffective. The exercise may be excellent, but if it's not built on previously established principles and information, it will not make any meaningful impact. Without a solid theoretical foundation, experiential learning loses some of its power (Furr, 2000). Content must be grounded in theory to have a logical progression among sessions (Furr & Fulkerson, 1982).

Components of Learning

Group sessions are composed of educational content that includes didactic, experiential, and processing components (Furr, 2000). Each session should incorporate at least one piece of content that includes all three components. In a group session that may last one hour or longer, these three components may be repeated when new content is introduced. In the didactic component of a session, leaders present and teach information. In the experiential component, group members take that new information and apply it through an activity. In the processing component, group members reflect on what they have learned and experienced, and how they might utilize that knowledge in their lives.

Didactic Component

A distinguishing factor of structured groups is their commitment to teaching psychological principles (Furr, 2000). Because structured groups are generally brief in terms of the number of sessions, members do not have time to discover all of the information for themselves. The didactic component "allows the leader to take a directive role in teaching information appropriate to the group topic" (p. 35). The leader must decide what information can be directly taught. It is assumed that the leader has some knowledge that members may not be able to discover through normal group interactions. With mini-lectures, the leader can provide the background knowledge needed for initiating the change process. Through presenting material in small segments, members can master material before engaging in activities based on this knowledge.

Didactic presentations incorporate open communication between the group leader and members (Furr, 2000). The leader should encourage comments and questions as a method of checking members' perceptual accuracy. Material should be presented using interactive methods so that members can respond immediately to the ideas discussed. Members should be actively involved in the lectures so that the information becomes more than just an intellectual exercise. Asking members to apply the information to personal life experiences is one way to evaluate whether the information has been perceived accurately.

Information is best presented in small segments (or mini-lectures), which can be reinforced through other activities (Furr, 2000). Each mini-lecture should provide an understanding of one step of a larger concept, and generally lasts between five and 15 minutes, depending on the age of the members. When the lecture portion of the group becomes too long, it likely indicates that too many concepts are being introduced at the same time. Information needs to be presented in small segments that prepare members for the experiential learning activities that follow. Each lecture segment is designed to build upon previous segments until the concept being introduced is fully examined. Didactic presentations begin with the simplest aspect of the concept and expand to more complex ideas. The leader must consider the knowledge level of the group members so that the content is neither too elementary nor too advanced. When the material is too easy for members, they can lose interest in the group, but if the material is too advanced, they may withdraw or feel threatened by the group.

Although the potential to learn new information may attract individuals to join the group, information alone is not enough to gain commitment to the group. Motivation and involvement decrease when the focus remains on information. Didactic information is a vital part of the group format, but the material discussed should be limited to the knowledge required for the experiential learning to be successful. The didactic component must blend with the experiential component for the group members to fully comprehend the concepts. Meaningful change—the goal of a structured group—is "dependent on the [member's] ability to apply the concepts to life situations" (Furr, 2000, p. 36).

Experiential Component

Experiential learning is the second component of useful educational content. The experiential component "allows the material [introduced in the didactic component] to be encountered on a personal level" (Furr, 2000, p. 36). In other words, it contextualizes it for independent, real-world use. After members have been exposed to new concepts, they need the opportunity to apply what they have learned through experiential activities (see Step 5: Exercise Design for information about how to create exercises that fulfill the experiential component of learning). Combining an intellectual or didactic component with an affective experience can be a powerful tool for facilitating change. When an issue or concept is experienced on a personal level, it becomes more relevant. An intellectual grasp may be necessary but is not sufficient to lead a person to action. To learn by doing rather than just by listening results in a deeper and more complex educational experience. As the individual becomes more involved in the learning process, they can take more responsibility for applying the information in a personal way.

The role of the leader in experiential learning is to determine the parameters for the experience. Whereas the leader maintains some "degree of control over the presentation of the didactic material, [they] can only determine the direction of the experience" (Furr, 2000, p. 36). Members may respond differently due to their own personal experiences with the topic. Therefore, the leader must anticipate the effects of the experience and determine where to place limits. Limits usually address the depth of the emotional exploration that will be encouraged by the exercise or activity. For example, in helping members to address messages about self-esteem, the leader could have them recall positive messages they had received at some point in their life or could have them write a positive letter to themselves that they wish they had received from a significant person. The first exercise would generally bring out some feelings of confidence, while the second one may evoke feelings of loss or sadness for the response they never received. It is imperative that the leader be aware of the impact of the exercise before introducing it to the group. Engaging members in meaningful experiences with properly placed limits increases member cohesion and commitment. Abstract concepts become personalized, and member confidence increases as they learn to apply new concepts.

Experiential activities also need to be linked to theory. These exercises can address each of the five dimensions (cognitive, behavioral, emotional, physical, and existential [see page 42]) , depending upon what aspects of development the theory addresses. The primary emphasis is on having members actively involved in applying the psychological concepts being taught. Members can retain a greater amount of the information they are taught if they can apply it to a personal situation. Members need to move from the position of information-having to a place of comprehension. The leader determines how the theoretical concept can be implemented practically through utilizing the experiential component.

The experiential component will affect each person in a different way, resulting in different outcomes for the members. Therefore, the leader must arrive at each session prepared to handle individual questions and reactions to the exercise (Furr, 2000). At times, the leader will encounter discrepancies between the intended purpose of an activity and the actual outcome for the members. The way in which the leader deals with these discrepancies is through the third element of the session content, which focuses on process.

Processing Component

The true meaning of the structured group comes from processing how the content and activities join together (Furr, 2000). After learning a concept that is then applied during the activity, the member needs to make sense of this experience. The processing component is what helps group members connect the experiential and didactic components. After the experiential learning has occurred, members may need to "clarify the conclusions they derived from the experience or examine questions that arose from the experience" (pp. 36–37). In this stage, the leader should prompt processing questions and discussions that help members link the experiential activity with theory, allowing them to generalize this experience to a broader life context. Consequently, the processing component becomes the link between the group experience and the individual's life outside of the group. Whereas the experiential personalizes a concept for the member, the processing component integrates the new awareness with the individual's perceptual framework. Even when an exercise is not completely successful, the leader can help members extract general principles that facilitate learning.

During the experiential component, the leader can note issues and concerns that arise for members. These issues and concerns can then be shared and examined during the processing component. An adequate amount of time must be devoted to processing for any piece of educational content to be impactful. Members must engage in processing so that they can integrate the didactic and experiential components. At this point, the leader can share observations about the actions and responses of group members. During processing, cognition and affect become fully integrated and assimilated into the individual's frame of reference. If the leader does not devote enough time to this component, the chance for transfer of learning decreases.

Although counselors engage in processing ideas with clients regularly, it is important that leaders, prior to a group session, carefully construct a couple of processing questions for each lesson that will lead to deeper understanding. These questions need to focus on linking the content and the activity. Avoid asking generic questions like, "What was this experience like for you?" Instead, ask focused questions like, "When you changed your negative statement to a coping statement, how were you affected emotionally?" Focused questions will better consolidate the experience. Additional questions could hone in on what barriers may come up during the week when trying to engage in more positive self-talk or what might help them believe their new positive statements. After leading a group several times, these questions may be refined and expanded upon to encourage members to probe for deeper understanding. Using the Socratic method of employing "what" and "how" questions can lead to deeper insights (Wharne, 2022). By adding these questions to the group manual, the leader will have access to provocative inquiries that will facilitate discussion. In addition to planned processing questions, leaders need to spontaneously create processing questions that fit the immediate context of the group. Unique learning opportunities will be presented by group members that the leader may not have anticipated.

By asking questions, leaders encourage members to take ownership of the material, thus shifting focus from the leader to the members (Furr, 2000). The members need to take the material and put it in their own words. It also provides the leader with the opportunity to detect any misconceptions or inaccuracies that may have occurred. When the leader adds questions about ways the members can apply these ideas outside of the group, it helps members focus on their goals for the week. Often, leaders will ask members to share what they plan to do before returning to the next group session. This type of processing serves two purposes. First, it creates awareness that members need to take action outside of group meetings to change. Second, making a public commitment to these actions creates an expectation that they will make a change. However, the leader must follow up on these commitments at the beginning of the next session. Reporting back to the group can become a powerful motivator for change.

As a word of caution, avoid allowing this processing time to evolve into a therapy group. Keep the focus on what was learned and how it is applied. There may be a temptation to probe deeper into emotions as they are shared, but such a pursuit can create a level of discomfort for other members who did not join the group for that purpose. Even the person who shared may approach the next group session with some trepidation after they have had time to reflect on their vulnerability from sharing.

Finally, be sure to allow adequate time for processing. It can be helpful to create a timeline for each component of the group and follow that plan. Some activities, such as art activities, can be time-consuming. However, a collage does not have to be completed to be meaningful. Being able to share the meaning derived from the activity is of greater importance. Let members know in advance when an activity will end so they have a timeframe. Providing an agenda for what will happen within the group allows members to know there will be time for sharing at the end. Processing allows the group to have a sense of completion for each objective and helps members move to the implementation of new learning between sessions.

Dimensions of Learning

There are many ways to incorporate the three components of learning (didactic, experiential, and processing) into each of the dimensions of learning (cognitive, behavioral, emotional, physical, and existential) (Furr, 2000). Different counseling theories focus on helping clients change in one of these areas. These sections have suggestions for how much time to spend in each learning component. However, these suggestions are just that: suggestions. The leader should make the final determination of how to utilize the time allocated for each component.

Cognitive

The cognitive dimension focuses on intellectual development and involves a large didactic component (60%). At times, the leader may illustrate a principle through an exercise, but the primary emphasis is on information. Processing at this stage is useful in checking the accuracy of the members' perceptions of the information. After information is presented, members try to apply it to their own situations. It is the leader's role to foster application of the information as a method of personalizing the knowledge gained from the lecture. Exercises are usually brief and at times conducted on an individual basis (15%). Members may be asked to fill out an inventory about their beliefs or to identify negative cognitions. After the experiential component, the leader actively initiates the processing through exploring the impact of these changes on their belief systems or thought processes (25%). The processing may initially take place in small sub-groups so that each member has the opportunity to examine their own experience and share conclusions with other group members. The leader may continue the processing with the total group as a means of identifying commonalities among the different group members.

If the goal is to change cognitions, more time may be spent on the experiential component. Theoretical approaches such as cognitive behavior therapy (CBT) and rational emotive behavior therapy (REBT) incorporate the idea of changing thoughts as a way of changing affect and behavior. Numerous exercises can be designed to modify cognitions, but these exercises still need to be preceded by a didactic component and summarized through a processing component. It may not be enough for an individual to understand intellectually that thoughts are a powerful influence on feelings and actions—the person also needs to experience the impact of changing these cognitions. Through structured exercises, the change can be implemented and then evaluated within the group.

Behavioral

When addressing the behavioral dimension, the goal is to change outward behavior rather than thoughts or covert behavior. A pure operant behavioral model would shape behavior by instigating a system of rewards, punishment, and response consequences. However, the approach generally taken in structured groups is to first instruct individuals in ways to change their behavior and then establish appropriate consequences for them to apply to themselves. The instruction or didactic component may include descriptions of the desired behavior as well as step-by-step explanations of how to acquire the behavior. The leader also may provide examples of the target behavior through models or role-plays. When a behavior is taught within a session, an equal amount of emphasis should be placed on the didactic (40%) and experiential components (40%). Members need an opportunity to rehearse the new behavior in a supportive atmosphere with accurate feedback. They should have a chance to make mistakes in a setting with minimal adverse consequences. If behavioral rehearsal is properly sequenced, members can learn new behaviors in small steps, thus maximizing the chances of success.

Processing at each step of the learning sequence allows the individual to self-evaluate on their progress (20%). As feedback is received from observers, the member can make appropriate modifications so that one step will be mastered before another is undertaken. During the processing component, leaders quickly become aware that emotional content evolves regardless of which dimension (cognitive, behavioral, emotional, physical, or existential) is being tapped. In the behavioral dimension, members may become frustrated with the amount of energy they need to invest for change to occur and may even get angry with themselves over past failures. Others could be frightened by the new opportunities and risks that accompany change. The leader must be prepared to deal with these affective responses without losing sight of the behavioral goals.

Emotional

In approaching the emotional dimension, it is important to acknowledge that emotional content does not exist in a vacuum. A strong cognitive component is part of any emotional experience because thoughts trigger emotional reactions, and there is a tendency to give cognitive labels to emotions. Emotions are generally experienced on a physical level and examined on a cognitive level. Talking about emotions removes them from a purely affective level and places them within a cognitive framework. Consequently, to prepare for the experiential component of a session in the emotional dimension, members need a significant didactic component (30%). Stating each experiential exercise's purpose clearly maximizes the benefits of that exercise. This is not to say that members should be told specifically what they will gain as they explore their feelings—that specificity is impossible to predict when dealing with emotions—but members should know at the onset that they may be touched on a particular emotional plane and should be warned about any discomfort or distress an experience may evoke. That way, members can make an informed choice about their level of involvement in the experience. For example, in a group focused on grief, the leader may want to explain the stages of grieving before concentrating on a particular stage. The leader may discuss possible reactions and permit members to end their participation at any point if emotions become overwhelming. Members are then prepared to enter the experience knowing what to expect and will be more willing to take risks.

The experiential component is crucial when dealing with affect (40%). The goal of this component is to help individuals examine emotions and resolve intrapersonal conflicts. Individuals need to gradually begin exploring affect, so the pacing and sequencing of events within this dimension are important. If the leader moves too quickly, members may become frightened and resist exposing their emotions. Some may take personal risks and be unprepared to deal with their ensuing emotional reactions. The role of the leader is to plan the content in a way that allows members to start with activities that are low in risk and build toward those experiences that require a greater degree of personal risk-taking. The leader must be familiar with the parameters of the group and be prepared to adjust the pace of the exercise so that it moves rapidly enough to challenge members, but slowly enough to accommodate their safety needs.

Because the focus of structured groups is not catharsis of emotions, processing the affective content is necessary for the experiential aspect to be effective (30%). Members need to put the emotional experience into a conceptual framework if it is to have a continued impact. Processing allows individuals a chance to resolve any aspect of the exercise that is unfinished for them. Affective exercises can be powerful, and the leader can use processing to follow up on individual responses to the exercises. Often, not enough attention is given to processing after members have experienced an emotional exercise. They may leave with unresolved, painful feelings that create discomfort between group sessions. Some may not return to the group, whereas others return with a new cautiousness. At times, leaders have been reluctant to process an exercise, believing the experience alone is enough and that meaning is lost if the experience is discussed. However, casualties following encounter groups need to serve as an indicator of the importance of processing. People need to reintegrate emotions and cognitions during the group before returning to their everyday environments. It can be helpful to check in with members at the end of a session to ensure any unexpected feelings have been addressed. Using a "round" at the end of each session can help members acknowledge what was gained in the session and what was a challenge.

The structured group is limited in the amount of therapeutic intervention which can occur; therefore, the leader's role is to establish boundaries around the depth of affective exploration. While it is tempting to probe emotional reactions to prompt members to go deeper, the goal of a structured group is to have members recognize feelings that accompany their issue. These groups are not a forum for deep exploration of feelings. Structured groups are not a replacement for in-depth individual and group therapy but are a supplement to these therapeutic approaches.

Physical

Psychological concepts can be connected to the body's physiological responses, making the physical dimension the primary group topic (didactic, 25%). Physiological responses often are cues to the emotional state of the individual. When a person loses awareness of their affective state, important body signals may also be ignored. Treatment in areas such as incest survival and eating disorders has found it beneficial to attend to the physical manifestations of these issues. Exercises directed toward examination of the physical side can help the individual more fully integrate all parts of the self. In fact, the body's responses may be a signal that an internal conflict exists and can serve as an early warning system for the individual. Body sensations may offer clues to the underlying emotional issues that are not readily available for discussion. It is important to recognize that a mind/body dichotomy does not exist, and all aspects of an individual are interrelated (Fehr, 1991; Motofei & Rowland, 2018).

By increasing physical awareness, the individual can better cope with other aspects of life. A majority of the emphasis in the design of a session in the physical dimension needs to be on experiential learning (50%). Some instruction may be necessary to help members connect their physical sensations, cognitions, and affect. However, the most effective method is letting people experience how their bodies respond physically to different stimuli. Members can learn to become more sensitive to subtle cues and physical sensations which leads to an understanding of their internal response patterns. After the experience has occurred, follow-up is needed to integrate the experience with the affect, thoughts, and behavior. Some exercises such as relaxation training have a clear direction and need little explanation. Processing (25%) may then concentrate on assisting individuals in applying the technique to other life situations. Other exercises such as the Gestalt body awareness activities may trigger affective responses and must be processed to move to a deeper level of understanding (Reynolds, 1996). The leader needs to be aware of possible connections between the physical dimension and the affective dimension. Without that awareness, exercises may trigger a more intense response than the leader or members expected. In general, most content focused on the physical dimension is highly experiential and needs only minimal didactic and processing components.

Existential

Finding personal meaning in life is the province of the existential dimension. Meaning cannot be taught but must be discovered through individual experience. Consequently, less time is devoted to didactic themes (20%) and more time is spent on the experiential (40%) and processing (40%) aspects. Because the existential viewpoint sees the individual as a three-part unity of body, mind, and spirit, exercises may incorporate exploration of several areas of self, with the primary focus on growth in consciousness. Development from the existential point of view contends with the individual transcending the self and becoming involved with others. The processing phase of the group is one way for individuals to gain an understanding of the self in relation to others. The experiential phase allows the member to address intrapersonal issues and conflicts. A balance is needed between the experiential and processing aspects for the individual to connect the intrapersonal view with a broader world perspective.

Few structured groups focus totally on existential development, but the leader will discover that existential issues are incorporated in the cognitive, behavioral, and emotional facets of the individual. Psychoeducational topics such as life stage transitions, career choice, and lifestyle enrichment acknowledge the importance of finding meaning in life and making a commitment to take responsibility for choice. In many instances, awareness must occur on the existential level before lasting change can be implemented on any of the other levels. The leader needs to recognize that any group exercise involving existential ideas must allow adequate time for the experience to develop naturally. The exercise itself should be directed toward finding meaning and allowing values to be examined and actualized. When a member encounters the deeper part of self that gives meaning to life, they need to share the experience with others to make the encounter complete. Enough time should be allotted for exploration of the experience and application of the ideas that evolve. Thus, the major portion of time is devoted to the experiential and processing aspects.

Dimensions of Learning by Components

All three components are essential to group functioning; however, there will be variation in terms of time allocated to each depending on the topic (Furr, 2000). The amount of time devoted to each of the three components depends on the dimension of change being addressed. There is a complex interaction between the five dimensions and the three components of learning. Figure 1 highlights the variance the leader may encounter as the different dimensions are addressed during the group. The left column indicates the dimension being addressed. To the right of each dimension are estimates of the percentage of time spent in each of the three components of learning. Each of the dimensions varies according to how much time is spent presenting didactic material, engaging in experiential activities, and summarizing through processing. All three components must be included, but will have different points of emphasis depending on which dimension is used. For example, when focusing on the cognitive dimension, 60% of the time may be spent on the didactic component, 15% is invested in the experiential area, and the remaining 25% is involved with processing. That means there is a large investment of time in teaching, but because the thought process is internal, the activity may focus on identifying thoughts and brainstorming how to change them. Then, the entire group shares how this process worked for them and any roadblocks they encountered. Some processing may also focus on how changing the thought impacted them on an emotional level. These guidelines are only suggestions and may vary according to the goals of the session. The idea is to address each dimension according to the inherent nature of that quality.

Figure 1

Dimensions of Learning by Components

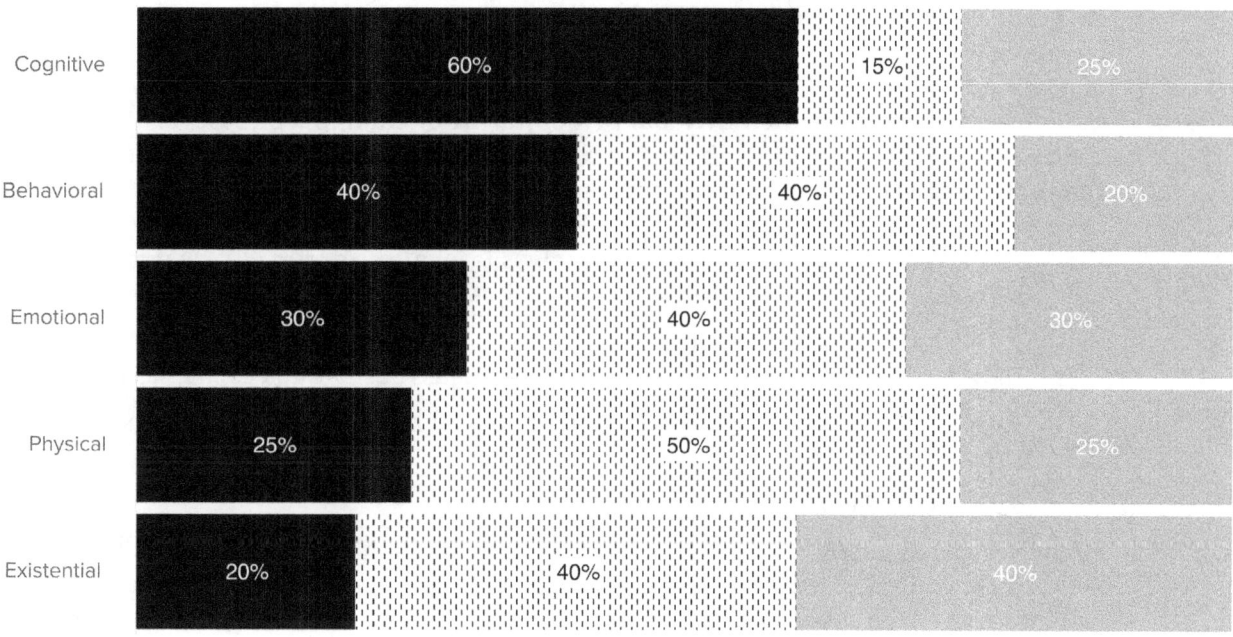

Legend: ■ Didactic Component ⁙ Experiential Component ▨ Processing Component

Dimension	Didactic	Experiential	Processing
Cognitive	60%	15%	25%
Behavioral	40%	40%	20%
Emotional	30%	40%	30%
Physical	25%	50%	25%
Existential	20%	40%	40%

Ask Yourself

Content is derived from the objectives that have been established for the group and includes the didactic, experiential, and processing components. These three components then are applied to the five individual dimensions of cognitive, behavioral, emotional, physical, and existential self. The emphasis of each of the three components will vary according to the dimension being addressed. But for any group design to be impactful, an appropriate balance of the three components is necessary or members will lose interest and withdraw from the group.

To complete Step 4, leaders should address the following questions:

1. What information needs to be presented didactically?
2. What learning experiences will personalize the information for the individual?
3. How much processing is needed to summarize the experience, and for transfer of learning to occur?
4. What dimension(s) (cognitive, behavioral, emotional, physical, or existential) will be addressed by the group?

EXAMPLE

Building Self-Esteem Group: Selection of Content

1. **Self-talk and self-esteem:** At this point, the notion of self-talk and its involvement in self-esteem are explained. The leader may begin by asking the group about their definition of self-esteem. The leader explains that what one says to oneself is the most accessible factor to an individual in monitoring or changing one's level of self-esteem. Have the group think about getting back a test paper with a poor grade and then ask them what things they say to themselves that keep them from maintaining their self-esteem. Define types of self-talk (negative, positive, coping). Emphasize that being aware of what they say to themselves is what the group will be working on in the remaining sessions. Explain the principle that changing self-talk changes feelings about oneself.

   a. Didactic: Distribute handout on self-talk and discuss positive and coping self-talk.

   b. Experiential: Lead a small group activity about changing negative statements to coping statements.

   c. Processing: Regroup and discuss.

2. **Homework assignment:** Ask the group to write down statements they make to themselves during the week that could be considered negative self-talk. For each negative self-statement, ask them to generate a coping restatement that does not decrease self-esteem. Again, re-emphasize the importance of doing the homework. Distribute homework forms.

EXAMPLE

Building Self-Esteem Group: Processing Questions

Based on the content selected in Step 4, leaders should ask the group the following processing questions:

1. How does your negative self-talk affect your feelings about yourself?

2. How did your feelings toward yourself change once you switched to a coping statement?

3. What difficulties might you encounter when trying to change self-talk as you go through your week?

4. What are some of the ways you can apply these principles during the next week?

Step 5: Experiential Exercise Design

Exercises are the driving force in effective structured groups. The content must be presented in such a manner that it impacts the individual in a meaningful and lasting way. There is a tremendous desire for information on psychological issues, as evidenced by the surge in the number of self-help books, with 85,253 books published between 2013 and 2019 (Pierce, 2021). In general, however, the knowledge gained from this information only affects the cognitive or intellectual dimension and does not expand to include other dimensions such as behavioral or emotional. Consequently, growth is limited and often short-lived.

Although exposure to information (also known as the didactic component of learning) is important, the member also needs to take ownership of that information and translate it into a personal frame of reference. This is where designing the experiential component enters the group planning process. As described in Step 4, each group session must contain all three components of learning (didactic, experiential, and processing). The experiential component refers to group exercises, which are the primary way of navigating the individual through the complex maze of thoughts, feelings, behaviors, and beliefs. Once you have completed Step 4 and selected the content for your group, you can move on to Step 5, in which you design aligned experiential activities (Furr & Fulkerson, 1982; Furr, 2000).

Exercise Categories

Many excellent exercises already exist and can be adapted to meet the needs of a particular group. Before choosing to use an exercise created by someone else, the leader must first recognize the theory and goals behind the exercise. To evaluate an exercise, the leader should consider several factors, such as the age and experience level of the participants, the amount of self-disclosure encouraged by the exercise, and the dimensions addressed by the experience. The exercise needs to be appropriate to age and experience levels, or the member will not have adequate developmental growth to benefit from the activity. If an exercise is too cognitively or emotionally advanced, members may either ignore it or distort it to match their own developmental level. The level of self-disclosure required by an exercise is critical to the success of an experience. Too much self-disclosure may result in members becoming resistant and refusing to complete the exercise, whereas too little self-disclosure may leave members feeling empty after the experience. Finally, the leader must be aware of the primary dimension affecting the members. If prior experiences in the group have attuned participants to the emotional dimension and the exercise addresses another dimension, such as cognitive, members may become frustrated by the incongruence. Although it is important to reach the members on these various dimensions, the leader needs to plan the components of the group to be congruent with the functioning level of the group members. Generally, cognitive aspects should be addressed before moving to the emotional. Therefore, the leader must examine the previous experience of the members, the level of self-disclosure desired, and the level of group functioning before deciding if an exercise meets the group's particular needs.

If an appropriate exercise does not exist, the leader can create an experience to address the issue at hand. Exercises do not have to be elaborate or complex to be effective. The leader must keep in mind the didactic-experiential-processing continuum and address at least one of the five dimensions. In some instances, an exercise may involve more than one dimension and should be appropriately sequenced so that one dimension prepares the individual to focus on the next dimension. Beginning with cognitions or behaviors, the leader then can move to more intimate issues involving emotions or meaning.

Teaching

Exercises can be grouped into several general categories according to the goals of the session. One category not commonly associated with exercises is teaching. The goal of teaching in a session is to eliminate learning deficits. This approach affects the cognitive dimension and is utilized in situations where the issue results from lack of information. It goes beyond the didactic component in that the material is actively incorporated into the members' frame of reference. The leader can use handouts that members read and discuss in the group, contracts to set individual goals, and homework to reinforce the ideas examined by the group. Contracting and homework also serve to implement changes on the behavioral dimension, illustrating that an exercise can address more than one dimension.

Creating games can be both a way of teaching new material and reviewing material already presented. Board games that follow the familiar format of popular games can be adapted to include new concepts. Utilizing a game show format is a fun way to review material from lectures and creates a competitive energy in the group. When using teaching as part of experiential learning, it is important for the leader to employ an interactive teaching style that allows time for questions, comments, and examples. Strategies that encourage member involvement increase the likelihood that information will be mastered.

Cognitive Restructuring

The immediate goal of cognitive restructuring exercises is to change self-talk and dispute irrational beliefs. Self-talk is defined as subvocal speech that usually serves to direct one's actions and evaluate one's behavior. It is the ongoing conversation with oneself that can arouse emotions or instigate action. One's beliefs are generally reflected in self-talk, and irrational beliefs can result in irrational affect and behavior. Modifying a client's cognitions creates changes in both the behavioral and emotional dimensions. As the client challenges irrational beliefs, they begin to respond differently to challenging situations. For example, obsessive thoughts about failure can trigger anxiety, which then impairs performance. But changing destructive beliefs can result in reduced anxiety and improved performance.

If an individual changes their thought pattern, both the affective reaction and behavior are modified. When the impact of cognitions is understood, self-talk becomes the target of an exercise. Members can monitor and subsequently change problematic self-statements. In approaching self-talk, the sequence of change is (1) recognition of inappropriate self-talk, (2) restructuring the content of self-talk, and (3) repeated implementation of the readjusted self-statements. Exercises need to include each of these components to be effective.

Role-Playing

The goal of role-playing is to facilitate behavior change, particularly in interpersonal situations. Role-playing allows members to rehearse new behaviors in a supportive environment and receive feedback in a constructive way. In any group where learning complex behaviors is the focus, role-playing is an effective tool.

An integral part of role-playing is feedback. Merely practicing the behavior is not enough. The member benefits from the reactions of other members and the comments of observers. Video recording the rehearsal of the behavior gives members the added advantage of self-observation. Members can choose to use their cell phones to record the role-play and then watch the behavior in the small group. By choosing to record, members are providing their informed consent. Strengths and areas for improvement can be discussed, and the behavior can even be practiced again. The leader can observe the small groups and provide additional feedback or respond to questions from members that arise from their role-plays. The leader may provide scenarios for members to practice, or members may create their own situations to rehearse. However, role-play activities are effective only when the individual is prepared to discriminate between appropriate and inappropriate behaviors. One way to teach discrimination skills is through modeling. The leader gives examples of both the desired target behavior and ineffective behaviors as a way of highlighting differences. It is important that the distinctions between the two types of behavior are clear, or members may mistakenly model the inappropriate behaviors.

The basic process followed in role-playing is modeling, imitation, repeated rehearsal, and generalization. The leader first provides examples of the behaviors. Then, members are given opportunities to reproduce the behavior while being observed and coached. When the basic principles are mastered, the behavior is rehearsed in a variety of situations until the member can generalize the behaviors to real-life experiences. One helpful tool the leader can provide is a rubric or rating scale that describes each component of the behavior. For example, the leader may create a rating scale for evaluating how well someone can say no to a request. The scale would include making eye contact, an assertive tone of voice, and the ability to refuse without making excuses. The observer can use this tool to provide consistent feedback to the person rehearsing the behavior. Eventually, members will be able to use the tool to provide feedback for themselves. Role-playing should do more than teach a behavior response; it should provide a safe environment for the individual to challenge previous beliefs and values, which may block behavior change. Although the main emphasis is on learning a new behavior, the leader must recognize that behaviors do not exist in isolation from thoughts and emotions. The leader needs to be attentive to the dimensions of role-playing exercises and to be aware when irrational thoughts or emotions interfere with learning new behavior.

Guided Imagery

Guided imagery is defined as a mind-body exercise that allows the client to simulate a demanding task to alter one's response (Sklare et al., 2003). These exercises can impact the behavioral area using covert rehearsal, in which a client imagines their improved behavior in a particular situation. Visualizing how one is supposed to act can actually improve performance. Its use in systematic desensitization is well-documented (Merrell, 2008), and these principles can be applied to the group setting. In this case, guided imagery involves both cognitions and affect because they both impact behavior (Özü, 2010). Imagining oneself in a particular setting can trigger an emotional reaction that may interfere with mastering the behavior. Consequently, the leader needs to be prepared to confront cognitions, affect, and beliefs that may be intertwined with the imagery experience.

Another use of imagery is to increase interpersonal awareness in both the cognitive and the existential dimensions. Suppressed emotions may be brought to the surface through reliving experiences, while life meaning may become clearer through fantasy exercises. The use of imagery allows the leader to transcend the physical limitations of the setting and results in a more personalized experience for each participant. In a sense, imagery serves to integrate the didactic experience with the five dimensions.

Creating Dichotomies

Psychological difficulties often emerge when an individual is caught between two desirable, but opposing options. To assist in resolving this type of conflict, exercises can focus on the creation of dichotomies, which highlight interpersonal inconsistencies. In these exercises, the member identifies areas in which conflicting ideas, beliefs, values, or actions exist. The member then explores each facet of the conflict and accepts responsibility for the contradictions. Members are urged to exaggerate these inconsistencies as opposed to minimizing the differences. In this way, tension increases and serves to move the person toward resolution of the incongruence. An example of this conflict is a group for adolescents who want to do well in school but also want to fit in with peers who devalue academic success. To do well in one aspect often means the other will suffer. By comparing the pros and cons of these two conflicting desires, the member can examine the conflict among values and examine the long-term impact of their choices.

Dichotomous exercises are particularly impactful in the emotional and existential dimensions. On the emotional level, the use of dichotomies can help resolve conflicting emotions and motivations.

Individuals are often immobilized by internalized conflicts and need to clarify the influence of opposing forces. Existential issues often are centered on finding truth and meaning in one's life. At times, this search is blocked because the individual confuses the real self with an image that they are trying to project. The use of dichotomies in an exercise can assist the individual in separating the real from the façade and then move the person toward self-acceptance. An example of this type of exercise is creating a mask with the outer side showing the public face and the inner side showing the real self.

Whenever an exercise employs dichotomies, both sides of the dichotomy need to be fully explored in a nonjudgmental atmosphere. Adequate time for processing must be provided. These exercises also bridge several dimensions that can create pacing and sequencing issues for the leader. The leader will have to decide how to address issues such as whether conflicting messages must be addressed before members can tackle emotional incongruencies (sequencing issues). Members may be able to resolve issues involving contradictory thoughts more quickly than issues centered on opposing values (pacing issues). Consequently, leaders utilizing exercises that incorporate dichotomies must be cautious in addressing more than one dimension at a time.

Creative Arts

Art, music, drama, and poetry offer innumerable ways to stimulate understanding and insight. Play therapy has paved the way for utilizing nonverbal ways of expression (Perryman et al., 2015). Art projects can include drawing/painting, sculpting, collage, film, and interpretation of existing art. Drawing can range from symbolic, such as a values shield—an activity in which participants fill in a four-section shield with four important personal values—to drawing images that compare pre- and post-situations. Sculpting with modeling clay can enable members to create something that represents a mood or value. Collaging is a useful activity for those who are not confident in their artistic talents. Members can use material from magazines to create an image that represents their deeper self. The use of current film clips may help illustrate a point and trigger a discussion of a current issue. Finally, the true value of art is that it is open to interpretation. Thus, the choice of a powerful piece of art that members interpret may be a way to explore meaning.

Music can be used to set the mood of the group, as background for other activities, and as a means of creating meaning through the words of a song. For adolescents, the choice of music is often a reflection of the issues faced by teenagers and can facilitate discussion of difficult topics. A group may want to choose a song that represents the meaning of the group and play it as part of the closing of each session. A song with deep meaning may offer an excellent tool for facilitating discussion of its meaning as applied to the group. When a song is chosen, it is the leader's responsibility to check the lyrics for appropriate content. Also, it is important to provide a copy of the lyrics for members to follow if the song is to be used as part of the activity.

Drama activities differ from role-play in scope and purpose. Role-play provides the opportunity for behavior rehearsal. Drama allows members to utilize scripts prepared prior to presentation. The leader may write a dialogue prior to the group for small groups to rehearse and present to the group. Much of the focus will be on the emotional content of the situation. Another approach is for small groups to write their own drama about the topic and present it to the group for discussion as a way of exploring emotional situations. Dramatic readings can also be used to enhance the material being presented.

Poetry can take either the form of reading a poem to the group or having members create their own poems. Using an established poem allows members to apply their own interpretation and meaning. Although most people would not think of themselves as poets, there are many structured formats that provide line-by-line guidance for how to write a poem. One such form is the diamante poem which gives instructions about how to write each line. Using this approach encourages members to express themselves in ways that are outside typical communication styles.

Journaling or writing activities can be included as a means of facilitating self-reflection or insight. These activities can be utilized either within the session and then discussed or as homework between sessions. Creating meaning from activities requires that new information be examined and placed in context. The parallel processes of assimilation and accommodation can only occur once the new information has been analyzed and infused into the member's current frame of reference, or when they can create a new way of viewing the situation. The member must make meaning of the experience by reflecting on the event and seeing where the experience fits with current beliefs. The importance of processing journaling activities must be emphasized. In the best scenario, journaling helps consolidate the learning experience. However, the member may uncover some unexpected thoughts or feelings that need to be examined within the group context for this new awareness to be incorporated into the member's perceptual framework. Reflecting on these writings within the group allows members to integrate the meaning being derived from the group with their experiences outside of the group.

Body Awareness

The focus of an exercise may be on the physical body and the way in which members interpret physical sensations. Body awareness exercises facilitate knowledge of physical signals that may be connected to behaviors and emotions. Relaxation exercises are a primary example of body awareness experiences. Other uses may include Gestalt awareness activities to create awareness of self. These approaches take the view that the body is inseparable from thoughts and feelings and hold the belief that awareness of physical sensations can lead to greater self-awareness. This technique can be useful when dealing with psychosomatic issues like anxiety management or changes that need to occur physically, such as weight reduction. Body awareness exercises can increase awareness of denied emotions and thoughts that are not in a person's conscious awareness. Becoming aware of physical sensations may lead to increased awareness of other dimensions.

Ask Yourself

The process of designing exercises is the most creative aspect of a structured group. Many types of activities have been successfully employed, and the approach is limited only by the creativity of the leader. Exercises may be directed at intrapersonal processes, group interaction, or subgroup sharing. Pacing and sequencing reflect the mood the leader wants to create. Exercises are essential to group effectiveness in that a well-designed exercise personalizes the content of the group and creates a desire for further growth.

Leaders should answer the following questions before designing an exercise:

1. Do previous learning experiences provide the foundation for the exercise?
2. Will the exercise reach individuals on the appropriate levels?
3. Do the exercises facilitate the proper amount of self-disclosure?
4. Will the exercise reinforce the didactic information?

EXAMPLE

Building Self-Esteem Group: Exercise Design

This exercise is designed to explore the relationship between self-talk and feelings about oneself. Its primary focus is on the cognitive dimension, as it impacts the emotional area. It contains didactic, experiential, and processing components.

1. **Distribute a handout on self-talk:** The handout contains examples of negative self-talk, which members then revise to create coping self-talk. In reviewing this didactic information, the leader may ask members to describe the differences between the types of self-talk. The leader may ask for personal examples of negative self-talk and demonstrate how to change these to coping self-talk.

2. **Small group activity:** The group is divided into triads and asked to state something that they typically say to themselves that reduces their self-esteem. The partners help the member in restating the self-talk in a way that does not decrease self-esteem.

3. **Regroup and discuss:** The leader asks the triads to share examples of negative statements and the revised coping statements.

Step 6: Reflection and Evaluation

Evaluation is an essential part of any structured group design (Furr & Fulkerson, 1982; Furr, 2000). For a group to be effective, the leader must test the ideas and determine what components facilitate change. Both the process and the outcome of the group need to be examined. Outcome evaluation refers to the degree of individual change experienced upon completion of the group, whereas process evaluation refers to the effectiveness of session-to-session activities. A group's effectiveness can only be determined after it has been implemented. A group design may look great on paper, but the true tests will be the response of the group members and whether it accomplishes what it intends to accomplish. If members do not change or grow in the desired direction, the group has not served its purpose. Consequently, outcome evaluation is necessary to assess whether participation has been beneficial to the members.

Outcome Evaluation

Outcome evaluation can take several forms. The most rigorous form is closely aligned with research design. Members are measured on objective criteria before entering the group and again after completing the group. Through these evaluations, members can see the measurable change and rate their own progress. This method is particularly applicable to groups with a specific focus, such as assertion training or weight management. It is more appropriate for groups that meet over a long period of time (ten or more weeks) because many of the changes take time to implement, whereas the focus of shorter groups is to plant ideas and give basic skills that can be translated into change in the future. These changes may not be evident after a short group, thus making it difficult to assess group outcome. In this situation, the focus may be on the evaluation of what content members learned. For example, members may be evaluated by their ability to change negative self-statements or by being able to demonstrate a relaxation technique.

A second form of outcome evaluation centers on the attainment of goals. At the onset of a structured group, the leader may ask individual members to establish their own goals and to record them for future reference. Upon completion of the group, members are asked to review their goals and evaluate their own progress in terms of their goals. This approach allows members to review the progress they have made and identify the changes they have implemented. Another benefit is that it teaches members to self-evaluate, a procedure that will assist them in maintaining the changes in the future. However, as with any measure of self-report, a halo effect may be evident (Westbury & King, 2024). If members enjoy the leader, they may report more changes than actually occurred. Therefore, making the goals more behavioral in scope increases the likelihood that members will be objective in reporting change.

Member satisfaction with the group is another common form of outcome evaluation. In this type of evaluation, members report their subjective reaction to the group rather than an objective outcome. They may evaluate the leader's style, the content of the group, and group activities. Member satisfaction reflects the degree to which members are attracted to the group. Those who find the group attractive generally become more committed to the group. For the change process to begin, participants must believe that the group will work for them. They need to perceive that they are receiving accurate information and that the leaders have a degree of expertise. They also need to see that exercises are appropriate and essential to the learning experience before they participate fully in the group. Satisfaction is not sufficient to create change, but it is a facilitative condition for nurturing change. Measuring member satisfaction is important if the leader wants to attract individuals to the group and keep them involved in group activities. However, measuring satisfaction does not indicate whether a group is successful.

Process Evaluation

Process evaluation is the second phase of measurement. It is an ongoing activity: Throughout the group, the leader should consult with members about how the group is progressing for them. Is the information presented in a way that meets the group's needs? Are the exercises helping members reach their goals? Do members need to revise their goals based on experiences in the group? One of the primary errors that leaders commit is staying tied to a group plan, even after it is no longer effective. Each group will be different, and the content may need to be slightly modified to meet individual needs. This issue does not mean that the entire group outline will be dropped, but rather that the leader is willing to alter the format to better meet the group's needs. The leader also must remember that it is impossible to meet every member's individual needs and must communicate this limitation at the beginning of the group.

Evaluation is closely related to the purpose, goals, and objectives of the group. These factors determine what outcome is to be evaluated. If this information is clearly stated at the beginning of the group, members will not have unrealistic expectations. The group outline should then meet the general needs of the group with only minor alterations. The goals and objectives provide an accurate way to evaluate outcomes because the group has an explicit purpose. If the outcome evaluation indicates that the group is not meeting the stated goals, then the leader needs to reexamine the initial purpose and instigate changes at that point. Process evaluation is a way to keep the group on target with the original purpose and goals. Although a structured group can have some flexibility, there are limits to the changes that can be made. If all the proper design steps have been followed and members are appropriately informed before the group, process evaluation will enhance the group experience by helping personalize the group for each participant.

Ask Yourself

Before beginning and upon ending the group, the leader must consider the following outcome evaluation questions:

1. How will the leader know if the group has been successful?
2. How will progress toward individual goals be measured?
3. How will member satisfaction be assessed?
4. How will the leader evaluate their performance?

During the group, the leader must consider the following process evaluation questions:

1. Is progress being made toward individual goals?
2. Are members benefiting from the content and exercises?
3. What do members want that has not been included thus far?
4. In what ways could the leader be more helpful to the group members?

EXAMPLE

Building Self-Esteem Group: Evaluation

Outcome Evaluation

1. Complete a pre-test with a measure of self-esteem and compare the results with a post-test score.
2. Have each participant set specific goals for how they want to change such as asking someone out for a date or speaking up in class. Evaluate whether the goal was reached.
3. Use the following questions as an indication of member satisfaction:

   a. To what degree were your goals met?
   b. How useful were the content and activities in helping you reach your goals?
   c. How would you rate the leader's performance?
   d. Were the leaders knowledgeable about the subject area, and did they communicate their ideas effectively?
   e. What was the most significant aspect of this group for you?
   f. What would you change about the group?

Process Evaluation

Throughout the group, the leader should ask the following questions:

1. Are these activities useful in helping you build your self-esteem, and if so, how are they useful? If not, what would you like to see changed?

2. Now that you've had experiences in the group, do you need to revise your original goals based on what you've learned so far?

3. What information do you need that you have not received at this point?

Step 4 Worksheet: Selection of Content

1. Based on the goal for the session, identify the objectives to be achieved.

2. Beginning with the first objective, outline the content to be covered. The content should be guided by the objective.

   a. What are the main points that members will need to understand to engage in learning activities? What definitions need to be presented?

   b. How can the leader elicit examples from members that illustrate the principles being presented?

c. What open-ended questions will facilitate members' engagement with the topic? (Some questions should be determined in advance, although the leader will create questions tailored to points made by members.)

d. How is the material personalized for each member? How are examples elicited from members in a way that helps them understand the concepts?

3. Repeat this process for each objective related to the goal for the session.

Step 5 Worksheet: Exercise Design

1. Determine the dimension you are addressing. The type of dimension influences the choice of activity. There needs to be congruence between the objective and the content of the activity. For example, if the focus is on cognitions, the activity needs to have a cognitive focus.

2. Consider if the activity needs to center on the individual and an internal focus or if it would benefit from interaction among group members. Does the activity need to involve the total group or would smaller groups such as dyads or triads provide more interaction among group members?

3. Align the activity with the content that precedes the activity. Does the activity flow naturally from what group members just learned?

Tip: Use a variety of activities to encourage participation. Members should come to the group with excitement about what new activities they will be doing. For example, role playing is not the only way to learn new behaviors.

Step 6 Worksheet: Outcome Evaluation

1. Is there an established measure of the concept of your group? For example, is there a measure of self-esteem that is reliable, and can it measure change that will take place over the length of time of your group?

2. Is your group topic amenable to members writing goals for changes they wish to make? How will they know they have made progress?

3. How important is member satisfaction? How can you distinguish between the group being a meaningful and impactful experience and the group just being an enjoyable social connection?

4. How can you determine what members have learned in the group and how they have applied this knowledge?

Step 6 Worksheet: Process Evaluation (use at the midpoint of the group)

1. How are you making progress toward your goals?

2. What content has been helpful? What have you learned?

3. What activities have you found useful?

4. What would you like to learn that we have not covered?

5. In what ways could the leader be more helpful to the group members?

Leadership

By following these steps, the conceptualization of the group leads to the development of logical and sequential group content. Each topic will be grounded in theory and support the next topic, like a scaffold. Designing this content takes time on the front end but creates a group that can easily be replicated over time or by others. The structured group manual needs to include both the content for the mini-lectures, as well as any directions and handouts for members. Equipped with a thorough manual, leaders may underestimate the importance of their leadership skills or become mechanical in delivering the content. Therefore, it is crucial to treat a group manual as a guide for the content, to infuse it with personal style, and to constantly adapt and update.

Leaders need to be so familiar with the material that they can put concepts into their own words rather than reading them from a script. It is beneficial to explore the group topic in depth before starting the group. A leader who does thorough background research on their group topic will have the depth of knowledge required to lead the group. They will also be equipped to answer questions that members might bring up that aren't covered in the manual. By the time leaders begin their group, they have invested a great deal of time in the design of the content, so they should be familiar with the information. However, leaders often adapt group manuals designed by other professionals and may benefit from reviewing the following checklist.

Structured Group Checklist

☐ Have I reviewed the group manual in its entirety before beginning the group?

☐ Have I determined if I plan to pre-screen potential members or utilize the first session for screening?

☐ Have I developed advertising materials that are accurate in describing the group or will I be dependent on referrals from other professionals?

☐ Am I thoroughly familiar with each session's content before leading the session?

☐ Have I made copies of all handouts prior to each session?

☐ If working with a co-leader, have we defined each person's role and the material they will present?

☐ Have I secured a working space that is free of distractions and that will provide adequate privacy?

The role of the leader of a structured group is somewhat different from the role of the leader in a counseling group. Because the leader is also an educator, the leader should be more active in sharing information than leaders of counseling or therapy groups would be. However, the leader needs to create a dialogue with the members so that they do not fall into a lecturing trap. Lectures are important, but they should not be the only event in a group. Often, members consider the leader an expert and may seek specific advice. Rather than giving answers to the members, the leader needs to encourage members to apply the lecture information to their own situations. The goal is to equip members with the skills to direct their own actions and make their own decisions. Therefore, the didactic sections must be interactive, with open-ended questions and engaging discussions about the topic.

The leader can employ many of the same skills used in other types of groups. Just as in a therapy group, establishing group rules and expectations is important in setting the tone of the group. Issues such as confidentiality are important to cover. It can be helpful to involve members in identifying rules that promote their own sense of safety. Because structured groups do not go into great depth in exploring emotions, the risks of emotional exposure are lower. Still, leaders must ensure that members understand that they have a choice in what they disclose. Even if members choose not to share, they still have ample opportunity to learn in structured groups. It is not unusual for a member to be quiet in the larger group but then engage in the smaller subgroup. Along with setting expectations, reviewing the goals and objectives of the group can be productive for the members, particularly if members did not go through an individual screening.

This process helps members evaluate if the group will be a good fit for them. Members must always have the option to leave the group, especially if they perceive a large discrepancy between the group's goals and their own expectations. At times, the initial group meeting serves as a type of screening in which leaders and members alike evaluate if the group is congruent with their needs. Here is an example of how an initial session could be organized.

EXAMPLE

Initial Session

1. Introduction.

   a. Leader welcomes members, gathers information about why members joined the group, and provides a brief overview of the group, including the statement of purpose, goals, and objectives.

   b. Leader guides an ice breaker activity and looks for commonalities among members.

   c. Leader establishes group rules and expectations and incorporates ideas from the members about how to create a sense of safety in the group.

2. Overview of current session.

   a. Leader presents an outline of what the group will cover in this session.

    b. Leader explains the didactic/experiential/processing sequence so that members have a clear understanding of what to expect in the session.

3. Didactic/experiential/processing sequence.

    a. Leader presents the first mini-lecture using an interactive teaching style that engages members in the group content for the session.

    b. Leader introduces first experiential activity. Members may be divided into small groups to engage in the activity. The leader may circulate among the small groups to see if they have questions or need support. The leader states how much time is allocated for this activity.

    c. Members return to the larger group to process the activity. Using predetermined processing questions, the leader engages the members in a discussion of what was learned in the small group activity. The goal is to help members identify key points and generalize how they will use the information outside of the group. This activity helps members connect the experiential activity with the content.

4. Conclusion.

    a. The end of the session includes a summary of the activities and what members learned that they can apply during the week. The leader may assign some type of "homework" activity to be completed before the next session. Often, the homework is to observe the behavior of others as related to the group topic.

        i. For example, in an assertion training group, members might observe how others speak up for themselves and what behaviors were effective.

    b. At times, the leader provides a worksheet to be completed and returned the next session. This is a time to answer any questions which were not addressed in the session.

To facilitate discussion during the session, skills such as linking are important, given that members are there for a common purpose (Milson, 2008). Demonstrating that the members face similar challenges or situations can help build group cohesion. Structured groups often begin with some sort of introductory activity in which members share their purpose for engaging in the group. That icebreaker conversation provides opportunities for linking. After separating the group into dyads or triads, the members return to the larger group to share their experiences, providing another opportunity for linking. Shared similarities can strengthen the group.

A similar format is followed in subsequent sessions. In the second session, it can be helpful to review the group rules to see if any modifications are needed. For example, in a school-based group, members may note that confidentiality has not been observed because some members have been discussing what occurred in the group with other students. Members may want to examine the consequences of violations of confidentiality. Another addition in subsequent sessions is to examine the impact of the homework assignment. Even if members do not complete the written assignment, any observations they experienced can be part of the discussion. If a homework assignment is not processed, members will not see the value of completing this activity in the future. The remainder of the session will follow the same format as the first session.

In all the sessions, active listening skills help create an atmosphere where members feel heard. Using skills such as restating and summarizing conveys that the leader is attending to the members.

Socratic questioning can lead members to deeper exploration (Gladding, 2020; Milson, 2008). This approach uses open-ended questions to probe in a way that stimulates critical thinking and guides deeper understanding. Though silence may create space for reflection, leaders should use it carefully and cautiously.

The final group session provides the opportunity to review the group experiences. It is not a time to introduce new material, but rather a time to reinforce learning and acknowledge growth. It is also an occasion for members to say goodbye to one another. This session may have a celebratory atmosphere, which allows members to appreciate what they have gained from the group experience. The session may have the following format.

Example

Final Session

1. Review of previous session and homework.
2. Focus on concluding the group.

   a. Review group goals and individual goals (if established at the beginning of the group).

      i. How well were members' goals met?

      ii. What were the members' biggest accomplishments in the group?

      iii. What would members have liked to have achieved but did not complete?

   b. Discuss goals for the future.

      i. Where do members go from here?

   c. Formal group evaluation.

   d. Closing goodbye ceremony. Members need to share appreciation for what they gained from other group members.

Members seem to appreciate the structure provided by the group and may experience discomfort if silence leads to an intense focus on a member or the expectation that the member explore deeper emotions. Psychoeducational groups differ in purpose from counseling groups, yet serve a vital role in helping clients grow and change. Members find that this unique approach can lead to increased understanding of self and improvement of interpersonal skills. By sharing content with other members who are experiencing similar life challenges, group members can see the universality of their struggles and experience the support of those who understand their challenges.

Conclusion

Structured or psychoeducational groups offer a vital role in helping clients grow and change. These groups differ from traditional counseling groups in various ways, one being the amount of preparation required for a well-designed group focused on teaching skills to clients and increasing perspective on specific client issues. Skilled leadership is needed, given that processing information is a vital part of the change process. Members are informed about the content in advance and have chosen to attend the group based on its focus, making it consumer-friendly. As a result, members feel empowered by the content they learn and the skills they develop. While designing the group can be labor-intensive, the leader will benefit from having an effective resource to facilitate client growth.

Structured groups are a valuable tool when working with clients who lack the knowledge and skills to deal with life's challenges. As counselors, we possess resources to facilitate client growth through providing instruction in a supportive environment. Through sharing ideas, our clients leave these groups equipped to engage in healthy approaches to their issues. From my experiences, the time needed to design a group is rewarding—group members appreciate the new skills and understanding they develop through participating in a group focused on their specific problem. Sharing this experience with others facing the same dilemmas provides encouragement and support. Plus, these groups are fun to lead. Through participating in creative activities, members can engage in the topic in a way that is exciting and rewarding. By creating a group that scaffolds from simple concepts to complex ideas, members learn to approach their issues without fear of failure.

Because structured groups are designed to be repeated, there may be concern that leading the same group topic could become boring. I have found that each group has its own uniqueness because members have different personal experiences with the topic. Although the leader follows the same format, constant adjustments must be made to incorporate individual needs into the format. Adjusting the group to fit the members is part of the art of leadership. One of the best compliments I received was from a member who stated that, although she knew that the group had a prepared structure, it felt like it had a natural flow. Most importantly, members leave with new ways of understanding their issues and innovative tools that help them break old patterns. The effort required to develop the group is rewarded through clients' positive responses. By employing this approach, counselors have an additional tool to support those who entrust us with their well-being.

References

American Psychological Association. (n.d.). *APA dictionary of psychology*. Retrieved October 30, 2025, from https://dictionary.apa.org/

Association for Specialists in Group Work. (1998). ASGW best practice guidelines. *Journal for Specialists in Group Work, 23*(3), 237–244. https://doi.org/10.1080/01933929808411397

Association for Specialists in Group Work. (2000). *Professional standards for the training of group workers*. https://cdn.prod.website-files.com/66eb2b42a65cb81a449a1675/6788419ea717bcf12841faf5_ASGW-Professional-Standards-for-the-Training-of-Group-Workers.pdf

Association for Specialists in Group Work (1998). ASGW best practice guidelines. *Journal for Specialists in Group Work, 23*, 237–244.

Bandura, A., Adams, N. E., & Beyer, J. (1977). Cognitive processes mediating behavioral change. *Journal of Personality and Social Psychology, 35*(3), 125–139. https://doi.org/10.1037/0022-3514.35.3.125

Beck, J. S. (2005). *Cognitive therapy for challenging problems: What to do when the basics don't work*. Guilford Press.

Bond, K., & Anderson, I. M. (2015). Psychoeducation for relapse prevention in bipolar disorder: A systematic review of efficacy in randomized controlled trials. *Bipolar Disorders, 17*(4), 349–362. https://doi.org/10.1111/bdi.12287

Capuzzi, D., & Stauffer, M. (2020). *Foundations of group counseling*. Pearson.

Cheek, D. K. (1976). *Assertive Black...puzzled White: A Black perspective on assertive behavior*. Impact Publishers.

Council for Accreditation of Counseling and Related Educational Programs. (2024). *2024 CACREP standards*. https://www.cacrep.org/for-programs/2024-cacrep-standards/

Curtis, D. F. (2014). Structured dyadic behavior therapy processes for ADHD intervention. *Psychotherapy, 51*(1), 110–116. https://doi.org/10.1037/a0033984

Day, K., Starbuck, R., & Petrakis, M. (2017). Family group interventions in an early psychosis program: A re-evaluation of practice after 10 years of service delivery. *International Journal of Social Psychiatry, 63*(5), 433–438. https://doi.org/10.1177/0020764017710301

De Jonge-Heesen, K. W., Rasing, S. P. A., Vermulst, A. A., Scholte, R. H. J., van Ettekoven, K. M., Engels, R. C. M. E., & Creemers, D. H. M. (2020). Randomized control trial testing the effectiveness of implemented depression prevention in high-risk adolescents. *BMC Medicine, 18*, Article 188. https://doi.org/10.1186/s12916-020-01656-0

Dewi, E. U., Nursalam, Mahmudah, & Yunitasari, E. (2023). The effect of peer support psychoeducation based on experiential learning on self-care demands among breast cancer patients with post-chemotherapy. *Journal of Public Health Research, 12*(1). https://doi.org/10.1177/22799036221146901

Ellis, A. (1997). Extending the goals of behavior therapy and of cognitive behavior therapy. *Behavior Therapy, 28*(3), 333–339. https://doi.org/10.1016/S0005-7894(97)80078-0

Fehr, F. S. (1991). Mind and body: An apparent perceptual error. *Journal of Mind and Behavior, 12*(3), 393–405.

Furr, S. (2000). Structuring the group experience: A format for designing psychoeducational groups. *The Journal for Specialists in Group Work, 25*(1), 29–49. https://doi.org/10.1080/01933920008411450

Furr, S., & Fulkerson, K. (1982, March). *Theory, design, and implementation of structured groups* [Paper presentation]. American Personnel and Guidance Association meeting, Detroit, MI, United States.

Gebhardt, H. M., Ammerman, B. A., Carter, S. P., & Stanley, I. H. (2022). Understanding suicide: Development and pilot evaluation of a single-session inpatient psychoeducation group. *Psychological Services, 19*(3), 423–430. https://doi.org/10.1037/ser0000543

Gladding, S. T. (2020). *Groups: A counseling specialty* (8th ed.). Pearson.

Gitterman, A., & Knight, C. (2016). Curriculum and psychoeducational groups: Opportunities and challenges. *Social Work, 61*(2), 103–110. https://doi.org/10.1093/sw/sww007

Hendriks, H., de Nooy, W., Gebhardt, W. A., & van den Putte, B. (2021). Causal effects of alcohol-related Facebook posts on drinking behavior: Longitudinal experimental study. *Journal of Medical Internet Research, 23*(11), Article e28237. https://doi.org/10.2196/28237

Joy, S., & Kolb, D. A. (2009). Are there cultural differences in learning style? *International Journal of Intercultural Relations, 33*(1), 69–85. https://doi.org/10.1016/j.ijintrel.2008.11.002

Kargin, M., & Hicdurmaz, D. (2020). Psychoeducation program for substance use disorder: Effect on relapse rate, social functioning, perceived wellness, and coping. *Journal of Psychosocial Nursing and Mental Health Services, 58*(8), 39–47. https://doi.org/10.3928/02793695-20200624-03

Keune, J. D., & Salter, E. (2022). From "what" to "how": Experiential learning in a graduate medicine for ethicists course. *Cambridge Quarterly of Healthcare Ethics, 31*(1), 131–140. https://doi.org/10.1017/S0963180121000876

Keyes, D., Turfe, H., & Das, J. M. (2025). *Prevention strategies*. StatPearls Publishing. Retrieved November 25, 2025, from https://www.ncbi.nlm.nih.gov/books/NBK537222/

Kolb, A. Y., Kolb, D. A., Passarelli, A., & Sharma, G. (2014). On becoming an experiential educator: The educator role profile. *Simulation & Gaming, 45*(2), 204–234. https://doi.org/10.1177/1046878114534383

Kolb, D. A. (1984). *Experiential learning: Experience as the source of learning and development*. Prentice Hall.

Maple, M., Wayland, S., Pearce, T., Sanford, R., & Bhullar, N. (2022). A psychoeducational support group for people who have attempted suicide: An open trial with promising preliminary findings. *Community Mental Health Journal, 58*, 1621–1629. https://doi.org/10.1007/s10597-022-00978-y

Merrell, K. W. (2008). *Helping students overcome depression and anxiety: A practical guide* (2nd edition). The Guilford Press.

Meyer, E. G., Battista, A., Sommerfeldt, J. M., West, J. C., Hamaoka, D., & Cozza, K. L. (2021). Experiential learning cycles as an effective means for teaching psychiatric clinical skills via repeated simulation in the psychiatry clerkship. *Academic Psychiatry, 45*, 150–158. https://doi.org/10.1007/s40596-020-01340-8

Milsom, A. (2018). Leading groups. In B. T. Erford (Ed.), *Group work* (2nd ed., pp. 86–111). Routledge. https://doi.org/10.4324/9781351110679-5

Miller, R. J., & Maellaro, R. (2016). Getting to the root of the problem in experiential learning: Using problem solving and collective reflection to improve learning outcomes. *Journal of Management Education, 40*(2), 170–193. https://doi.org/10.1177/1052562915623822

Motofei, I. G., & Rowland, D. L. (2018). The mind-body problem—three equations and one solution represented by immaterial-material data. *Journal of Mind and Medical Sciences, 5*(1), 59–69. https://doi.org/10.22543/7674.51.P5969

Mueller, C. M., & Dweck, C. S. (1998). Praise for intelligence can undermine children's motivation and performance. *Journal of Personality and Social Psychology, 75*(1), 33–52. https://doi.org/10.1037/0022-3514.75.1.33

Özü, Ö. (2010). Guided imagery as a psychotherapeutic mind-body intervention in health psychology: A brief review of efficacy research. *Europe's Journal of Psychology, 6*(4), 227–237. https://doi.org/10.5964/ejop.v6i4.232

Perryman, K. L., Moss, R., & Cochran, K. (2015). Child-centered expressive arts and play therapy: School groups for at-risk adolescent girls. *International Journal of Play Therapy, 24*(4), 205–220. https://doi.org/10.1037/a0039764

Pierce, D. (2021, March 9). Self-help books fill a burgeoning need. *Library Journal.* https://www.libraryjournal.com/story/self-help-books-fill-a-burgeoning-need

Reynolds, F. (1996). Working with movement as a metaphor: Understanding the therapeutic impact of physical exercise from a Gestalt perspective. *Counselling Psychology Quarterly, 9*(4), 383–390. https://doi.org/10.1080/09515079608258716

Sachs, G., & Erfurth, A. (2021). Predicting functional outcome in bipolar patients: Effects of cognitive psychoeducational group therapy after 12 months. *European Psychiatry, 64*(S1), S81–S81. https://doi.org/10.1192/j.eurpsy.2021.244

Şahin, H., & Türk, F. (2021). The impact of cognitive-behavioral group psycho-education program on psychological resilience, irrational beliefs, and well-being. *Journal of Rational-Emotive & Cognitive-Behavior Therapy, 39*, 672–694. https://doi.org/10.1007/s10942-021-00392-5

Shapiro, J. P., Burgoon, J. D., Welker, C. J., & Clough, J. B. (2002). Evaluation of the Peacemakers program: School-based violence prevention for students in grades four through eight. *Psychology in the Schools, 39*(1), 87–100. https://doi.org/10.1002/pits.10040

Singh, V., Kumar, A., & Gupta, S. (2022). Mental health prevention and promotion: A narrative review. *Frontiers in Psychiatry, 13*, Article 898009. https://doi.org/10.3389/fpsyt.2022.898009

Skeffington, P. M., Rees, C. S., & Kane, R. (2013). The primary prevention of PTSD: A systematic review. *Journal of Trauma & Dissociation, 14*(4), 404–422. https://doi.org/10.1080/15299732.2012.753653

Sklare, G. B., Sabella, R. A., & Petrosko, J. M. (2003). A preliminary study of the effects of group solution-focused guided imagery on recurring individual problems. *The Journal for Specialists in Group Work, 28*(4), 370–381. https://doi.org/10.1177/01933922030284009

Söchting, I. (2014). *Cognitive behavioral group therapy: Challenges and opportunities.* Wiley-Blackwell. https://doi.org/10.1002/9781118510261

Steinhardt, M., & Dolbier, C. (2008). Evaluation of a resilience intervention to enhance coping strategies and protective factors and decrease symptomatology. *Journal of American College Health, 56*(4), 445–453. https://doi.org/10.3200/JACH.56.44.445-454

Tapias, E., Coromina, M., Grases, N., & Ochoa, S. (2021). Psychological treatments with children of parents with mental illness: A systematic review. *Child & Youth Care Forum*, *50*, 1107–1130. https://doi.org/10.1007/s10566-021-09608-2

Terrazas-Carrillo, E., & Garcia, E. (2024). Initial outcomes for a stress management psychoeducational group for Latino college students. *Journal of College Student Mental Health*, *38*(1), 77–88. https://doi.org/10.1080/87568225.2022.2133044

Thomas, D. V., & Looney, S. W. (2004). Effectiveness of a comprehensive psychoeducational intervention with pregnant and parenting adolescents: A pilot study. *Journal of Child and Adolescent Psychiatric Nursing*, *17*(2), 66–77. https://doi.org/10.1111/j.1744-6171.2004.00066.x

Usta, E., & Aygin, D. (2020). Prospective randomized trial on effects of structured training and counseling on depression, body image, and quality of life. *Bariatric Surgical Practice and Patient Care*, *15*(2), 55–62. https://doi.org/10.1089/bari.2019.0028

Valls, È., Bonnín, C. M., Torres, I., Brat, M., Prime-Tous, M., Morilla, I., Segú, X., Solé, B., Torrent, C., Vieta, E., Martínez-Arán, A., Reinares, M., & Sánchez-Moreno, J. (2022). Efficacy of an integrative approach for bipolar disorder: Preliminary results from a randomized controlled trial. *Psychological Medicine*, *52*(16), 4094–4105. https://doi.org/10.1017/S0033291721001057

Volungis, A. M. (2020). The Signs of Suicide (SOS) Prevention Program pilot study: High school implementation recommendations. *North American Journal of Psychology*, *22*(3), 455–468. https://digitalcommons.assumption.edu/psychology-faculty/21

Westbury, C., & King, D. (2024). A constant error, revisited: A new explanation of the halo effect. *Cognitive Science*, *48*(12), Article e70022. https://doi.org/10.1111/cogs.70022

Wharne, S. (2022). Socratic questioning and irony in psychotherapeutic practices. *Journal of Contemporary Psychotherapy*, *52*, 137–144. https://doi.org/10.1007/s10879-021-09514-7

World Health Organization. (2004). *Prevention of mental disorders: Effective interventions and policy options. Summary report*. World Health Organization, Department of Mental Health and Substance Abuse/Prevention Research Centre of the Universities of Nijmegen and Maastricht. https://iris.who.int/server/api/core/bitstreams/ee5f57e7-4e22-4082-9cee-678ad97c406c/content

Yalom, I. D. (1995). *The theory and practice of group psychotherapy* (4th ed.). Basic Books.

Yalom, I. D., & Leszcz, M. (2020). *The theory and practice of group psychotherapy* (6th ed.). Basic Books.

Yen, S., Ranney, M. L., Tezanos, K. M., Chuong, A., Kahler, C. W., Solomon, J. B., & Spirito, A. (2019). Skills to enhance positivity in suicidal adolescents: Results from an open development trial. *Behavior Modification*, *43*(2), 202–221. https://doi.org/10.1177/0145445517748559

www.ingramcontent.com/pod-product-compliance
Lightning Source LLC
Jackson TN
JSHW061155200226
98169JS00004B/2